Between Sundays

Between Sundays

Daily Bible Readings

Based on the Revised Common Lectionary

Gail Ramshaw

Between Sundays
Daily Bible Readings Based on the Revised Common Lectionary

Editors: Samuel Torvend & Linda Parriott
Book Design: Circus Design
Cover Design: Michael Mihelich
Art: Tanja Butler

Library of Congress Cataloging-in-Publication Data
Ramshaw, Gail, 1947–
    Between Sundays : daily Bible readings based on the Revised common lectionary / Gail Ramshaw.
      p.   cm.
    Includes index.
    ISBN 0-8066-3590-8 (alk. paper)
    1. Bible—devotional use. 2. Bible—Reading. 3. Common lectionary (1992) I. Title.
BS617.8.R36 1997
242'.2—dc21
                                        97-21553
                                              CIP

Manufactured in the U.S.A.   ISBN 0-8066-3590-8   3-401

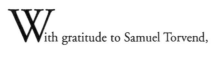

With gratitude to Samuel Torvend,

expert editor,

one of God's gardeners

Contents

Introduction

Daily Bible Reading

Many Christians have treasured the practice of daily Bible reading. Following the Reformation, family Bible reading became commonplace, and in the United States during the nineteenth century, the Bible was read daily in the public schools. Even Quakers, who did not read the Bible at First Day meeting, were expected to read it daily at home, so that when the community assembled for meeting, the Spirit would have something to work with. For Christians, daily Bible reading is not merely continual connection to a religious classic. Rather, since Christians believe that the Bible contains the word of God and conveys to us God's grace, Christians read the Bible in order to encounter Christ.

Perhaps a habit of daily Bible reading is more important now than in the past, for Christians can no longer assume that a majority of their neighbors and friends know the Bible and honor it. The church cannot absorb the Bible by osmosis from the culture around it. Rather, the baptized need to attend to the tasks of reading the Bible, learning to know it inside and out, encountering God's mercy in its pages, discussing its meaning for our time and comparing it with sacred books of other traditions. Daily scripture reading is one way to keep ourselves connected to the Bible and to reimmerse ourselves in the story of the God it proclaims.

Most people discover that simply reading straight through the Bible, Genesis to Revelation, is not the most helpful way to approach the scriptures. Even Augustine talks about the Bible as "of mountainous difficulty and enveloped in mysteries." Some readers get half-way through Leviticus and, rightly asking what in the world this has to do with them, abandon their endeavor. Despite that people talk about the Bible as if it were one book, it contains 66 books, plus the inter-testamental books, written in different times by different authors, and some individual books were compiled from material of different dates and situations. It is not surprising that people need some kind of plan for reading through this library. Many schedules for daily Bible reading are available, and each has something to commend it.

The Bible around Christ

Before there were inexpensive printed Bibles, Christians had ways other than daily Bible reading to learn the stories of their faith. One way was their use of the remarkable books called *Biblia Pauperum,* which, at first hand-drawn and later produced as blockbooks, circulated around Europe from the thirteenth through the sixteenth centuries. The *Biblia Pauperum* were picture books with captions. The center of each page depicted an episode from the life of Jesus, and around that picture were drawn stories from the Old Testament, which in some way illumined or paralleled or contrasted with the story of Jesus. According to this way of interpreting the Bible, the church understands the whole of the Bible as standing in relation to its central story for Christians: the life, death, and resurrection of Christ. That is, the primary goal for Christians is not necessarily historical knowledge of the ancient Near East, or comparison of its content with that of other religious books. Rather, Christians join in the tradition of all those people who told stories of God's salvation, and the church recognizes in the stories and images from the entire Bible examples of the divine grace and mercy it sees most fully in Christ.

This does not mean that Old Testament prophets were talking about Jesus. Nor does it mean that everything before Jesus was deficient. Quite the contrary. It is rather to say that just as Jesus fed the people with loaves and fishes, so God had fed the people with manna. Or again: it is not that the passover lamb was not "about" Jesus; however, learning about the passover lamb will teach Christians a good deal about what the New Testament says about Christ. Theologians teach that "scripture interprets scripture": that is, biblical writers used the language and imagery of earlier sacred books in order to tell their own stories of grace. The more we know of all these passages, the better we can interpret the ones we hear on Sunday morning.

This Daily Lectionary

This lectionary is inspired by those old picture books. It suggests that since the entire Bible contains the word of God Christians hear most clearly in the gospel, reading through the Bible book by book, verse by verse, isn't necessary—the Christian can read the entire Bible with one eye to Christ. Accordingly, this plan is based on the assembly's gospel readings, specifically on the Sunday readings of the Revised Common Lectionary.

For worshiping Christians the days of each week flow out from Sunday, the first day of the week and the day of Christ's resurrection. Whether we are present or not, the assembly of believers meet for Christian worship and read the appointed readings. The community gathers around Christ as revealed in the scriptures. Where the three-year lectionary is used, the liturgy presents us with a cluster of images about Christ: a gospel reading is at the center,

and around it are two other readings, a psalm, several hymns, a sermon, and prayers, perhaps also an offertory verse or a proper preface or choir anthem, a bulletin cover or appropriate banners. This daily lectionary enlarges the images by adding six more readings to encircle Sunday.

The Revised Common Lectionary is used now by many Protestants, including Lutherans, Methodists, Presbyterians, and members of the United Church of Christ. The Episcopalian lectionary and the Roman Catholic lectionary are closely related systems, for all three lectionaries are derived from the same source, the 1969 *Ordo Lectionum Missae*. In these three-year lectionaries, each week's selections follow the pattern of Luke's account of the Emmaus walk. To proclaim the resurrection, Jesus interprets Moses and the prophets to the disciples.

This daily lectionary extends such a Sunday hermeneutical technique throughout the week. The daily Bible readings expound further on the Sunday gospel reading, sometimes by providing background to the gospel's references and images, other times by reviewing other Old Testament stories that record God's good news, or by exploring additional epistles. Some of the most famous stories in the Old Testament and the Acts of the Apostles occur seldom in the Sunday lectionary, and some never; it is good to encounter these grand narratives during a week when they enhance the gospel reading.

The Gospel

The centerpiece of the three-year Sunday lectionary is the gospel. The Gospel of John, which records seven "signs" of Jesus with long accompanying discourses, is read mainly at the major festivals of the year and for significant liturgical events, such as the series of Lenten pre-baptismal Sundays in Year A. On most of the other Sundays of Year A, the Gospel of Matthew is read; in Year B, Mark; and in Year C, Luke.

This daily lectionary provides one other reading from a gospel each week, usually on Wednesday. That reading is either (1) a part of the year's gospel that is not included in the Sunday selections; (2) a part of the year's gospel that illumines or parallels the Sunday gospel; or (3) a reading from one of the other three gospels, especially John, that illumines or parallels the Sunday reading.

The First Reading

In the Revised Common Lectionary, the first reading during the festival half of the church year, from the beginning of Advent through Trinity, closely relates to the gospel reading. Throughout the Pentecost season, one track of appointed readings provides an Old Testament reading that in some way relates to the gospel reading. Another track of readings appoints scriptures in a more continuous fashion.

In keeping with the guiding principle that the gospel reading gives each week its focus, this daily lectionary appoints three of its weekly readings from the Old Testament to illumine or parallel the Sunday gospel. The selections may include (1) a narrative that illustrates the action of God as proclaimed in the gospel reading; (2) a story similar to the gospel narrative; (3) a selection that is background for and necessary to our understanding the gospel reading; (4) a poem from the Writings—Psalms, Wisdom literature, and other books—or a passage from the Prophets using imagery central to the gospel reading; or (5) an extended narrative connected to the Sunday's first reading. Sometimes the readings of Monday and Tuesday are two parts of a long Old Testament narrative that relates to Sunday's gospel reading.

The Psalm

In the three-year lectionary, the appointed psalm corresponds to the first reading.

In this daily lectionary, one reading each week, usually on Saturday, is taken from Psalms. Usually this psalm has been chosen because it expresses similar themes or employs similar imagery to the gospel reading. It may be the psalm cited in one of the Sunday readings. Nearly all 150 psalms are represented in the combination of Sundays and this daily lectionary.

Some persons who will use this daily lectionary already have the pattern of praying a daily psalm. This psalm might be either the psalm appointed for the past Sunday or the one suggested for Saturday. For their Saturday reading, these persons do best to replace the Saturday psalm selection with the next day's Sunday gospel. In this way Saturday anticipates the next Sunday readings, while Monday through Friday reflect upon the past Sunday readings.

The Second Reading

In the three-year lectionary, the second reading, taken from the New Testament letters and the Book of Revelation, can be one of two types. During the festival half of the church year, the second reading parallels or illumines the gospel reading. During the weeks after Pentecost, the second reading progresses through individual New Testament books one by one, covering their major passages week by week. This is called semicontinuous reading.

In this daily lectionary, one reading from the non-gospel portions of the New Testament is appointed, usually for Friday. This reading is either (1) a reading from another part of the New Testament which illumines or parallels the Sunday gospel or (2) a part of the book that is omitted from the Sunday semicontinuous readings.

How to Use This Lectionary

One way to use this daily lectionary is to read each day the suggested selection at meal time or in the early morning or before bedtime. This can be done either privately or with one's household, with or without prayer and hymnsinging. Some Christians use their time commuting to work on public transportation as a handy time for such daily prayer. Some practice a full form of morning or evening prayer, as found in their denominational worship resources, and will want to use this lectionary selection as the scripture reading. Any of the six readings may be read any day. Two or three readings can be combined for a midweek service, the only concern being that if Monday's and Tuesday's readings are a set, the sense of their connection to the Sunday reading be retained. Some persons may choose to read towards the coming Sunday, rather than out of the past Sunday. To do this, read the selections one week ahead.

Here is a simple order of daily prayer:
- a hymn, proper to the week, season, or time of day
- a Bible reading
- a moment of reflection
- a prayer for those in need and for one's self

Denominational resources, readily available, provide a wealth of suggestions to enrich this form with materials proper to the season and the week.

Finally, it is important to note that Christians observe not only Sundays, but also a calendar of festivals and commemorations. The churches using the Revised Common Lectionary have appointed different calendars of observances, and these calendars are not tied to the Sunday lectionary or to liturgical seasons. Some of these commemorations are included in the Revised Common Lectionary, such as Holy Cross Day, September 14. Some days are observed by some denominations, but not all, such as Mary Magdalene's Day on July 22. There is also Thanksgiving Day, dated by the secular calendar. Those Christians who wish to mark such observances in their daily prayer should feel free on these specific days to substitute for the daily lectionary selections the readings as appointed by their church, or use the readings in the section called "Lesser Festivals" at the end of this book.

If a reader were to highlight the Sunday and festival readings of the Revised Common Lectionary, he or she would be astonished how very little of the Bible gets read over the three-year Sunday cycle. Any course of daily Bible reading will acquaint the reader with more of the Bible than the Sunday readings can. This particular daily lectionary will do so in such a way as to strengthen one's reception of the Sunday readings themselves. This schedule allows Sunday to begin not only our week, but our week's reading through the Bible as well. We gather at the Tree of Life on Sunday, and we circle around it all week long. Our Sunday focus on Christ centers us in the Christian community; with this lectionary of daily Bible reading we stay connected to that Sunday until the next Sunday comes around.

Cycle A

Cycle A

First Sunday in Advent

SUNDAY	Isaiah 2:1-5	*War transformed into peace*
	Psalm 122	*Gladness in the LORD's house*
	Romans 13:11-14	*Salvation is near, wake from sleep*
	Matthew 24:36-44	*The sudden coming of salvation*
MONDAY	Genesis 6:11-22	*The flood is coming*
TUESDAY	Genesis 8:1-19; 9:8-13	*God saves Noah and the animals*
WEDNESDAY	Matthew 24:23-35	*The end is coming*
THURSDAY	Isaiah 54:4-10	*God will save the people*
FRIDAY	Hebrews 11:1-7, 32-40	*By faith Noah was saved*
SATURDAY	Psalm 124	*We have escaped like a bird*

Second Sunday in Advent

SUNDAY	Isaiah 11:1-10	*A ruler brings justice and peace*
	Psalm 72:1-7, 18-19	*The righteous shall flourish*
	Romans 15:4-13	*Living in harmony*
	Matthew 3:1-12	*Prepare the way of the Lord*
MONDAY	Isaiah 24:1-16a	*Judgment is coming, yet glorify God*
TUESDAY	Isaiah 40:1-11	*A voice crying in the wilderness*
WEDNESDAY	Matthew 12:33-37	*A good tree bears good fruit*
THURSDAY	Genesis 15:1-18	*God's covenant with Abraham*
FRIDAY	Acts 13:16-33a	*Paul preaches about John the Baptist*
SATURDAY	Psalm 21	*God comes with judgment and strength*

Third Sunday in Advent

SUNDAY	Isaiah 35:1-10	*The desert blooms*
	Psalm 146:5-10	*God lifts up those bowed down*
	or Luke 1:47-55	*My spirit rejoices in God my Savior*
	James 5:7-10	*Patience until the coming of the Lord*
	Matthew 11:2-11	*The forerunner of Christ*
MONDAY	Isaiah 29:17-24	*The infirm will be healed*
TUESDAY	Ezekiel 47:1-12	*The wilderness will flower*
WEDNESDAY	Matthew 8:14-17, 28-34	*Jesus heals*
THURSDAY	Zechariah 8:1-17	*God's promises to Zion*
FRIDAY	Acts 5:12-16	*Many people healed by the apostles*
SATURDAY	Psalm 42	*Hope in God*

Fourth Sunday in Advent

SUNDAY	Isaiah 7:10-16	*The sign of Immanuel*
	Psalm 80:1-7, 17-19	*Show the light of your countenance*
	Romans 1:1-7	*Paul's greeting to the church at Rome*
	Matthew 1:18-25	*Our God near at hand*
MONDAY	Genesis 17:15-22	*God promises Sarai a son*
TUESDAY	Genesis 21:1-21	*God saves Hagar and Ishmael*
WEDNESDAY	Matthew 1:1-17	*Matthew's genealogy*
THURSDAY	Genesis 37:2-11	*Joseph dreams*
FRIDAY	Galatians 3:23—4:7	*Paul writes of Jesus' birth*
SATURDAY	Luke 1:46-55	*Mary's song of praise*

Christmas

The Nativity of Our Lord | Christmas Eve

DECEMBER 24	Isaiah 9:2-7	*A child is born for us*
	Psalm 96	*Let the earth be glad*
	Titus 2:11-14	*The grace of God has appeared*
	Luke 2:1-14 [15-20]	*God with us*

The Nativity of Our Lord | Christmas Dawn

DECEMBER 25	Isaiah 62:6-12	*God comes to restore the people*
	Psalm 97	*Light springs up for the righteous*
	Titus 3:4-7	*Saved through water and the Spirit*
	Luke 2:[1-7] 8-20	*The birth of the Messiah revealed to shepherds*

The Nativity of Our Lord | Christmas Day

DECEMBER 25	Isaiah 52:7-10	*Heralds announce God's salvation*
	Psalm 98	*The victory of our God*
	Hebrews 1:1-4 [5-12]	*God has spoken by a son*
	John 1:1-14	*The Word became flesh*
DECEMBER 26	Luke 2:1-20	*Luke's story of Jesus' birth*
DECEMBER 27	Isaiah 9:2b-7	*The names of the coming one*
DECEMBER 28	Psalm 96	*The trees sing for joy*
DECEMBER 29	Genesis 1:1—2:4a	*The first creation story*
DECEMBER 30	Psalm 97	*Light dawns on the righteous*
DECEMBER 31	Titus 2:11—3:7	*The life of those reborn*

The Name of Jesus

JANUARY 1	Numbers 6:22-27	*The Aaronic blessing*
	Psalm 8	*How exalted is your name*
	Galatians 4:4-7	*We are no longer slaves*
	or Philippians 2:5-11	*God takes on human form*
	Luke 2:15-21	*The child is named Jesus*

First Sunday after Christmas

SUNDAY	Isaiah 63:7-9	*Israel saved by God's own presence*
	Psalm 148	*God's splendor is over earth and heaven*
	Hebrews 2:10-18	*Christ frees humankind*
	Matthew 2:13-23	*The slaughter of innocent children*
MONDAY	Hosea 11:1-11	*God's care for Israel*
TUESDAY	Jeremiah 31:15-22	*God's care for Ephraim*
WEDNESDAY	Matthew 13:54-58	*Jesus rejected*
THURSDAY	Exodus 1:15—2:10	*God saves Moses from Pharaoh*
FRIDAY	Hebrews 11:23-28, 32-40	*By faith Moses was saved*
SATURDAY	Psalm 71:1-16	*Prayer for deliverance*

Second Sunday after Christmas

SUNDAY	Jeremiah 31:7-14	*Joy as God's scattered flock gathers*
	Psalm 147:12-20	*Praising God in Zion*
	or Sirach 24:1-12	*Wisdom lives among God's people*
	Wisdom 10:15-21	*Praising the holy name*
	Ephesians 1:3-14	*The will of God made known in Christ*
	John 1:[1-9] 10-18	*God with us*

Epiphany

The Epiphany of Our Lord

JANUARY 6	Isaiah 60:1-6	*Nations come to the light*
	Psalm 72:1-7, 10-14	*All shall bow down*
	Ephesians 3:1-12	*The gospel's promise for all*
	Matthew 2:1-12	*Christ revealed to the nations*
JANUARY 7	1 Kings 10:1-13	*The Queen of Sheba visits Solomon*
JANUARY 8	1 Kings 10:14-25	*The wealth and wisdom of King Solomon*
JANUARY 9	Luke 13:31-35	*Receiving or rejecting Christ*
JANUARY 10	Micah 5:2-9	*The promise concerning Bethlehem*
JANUARY 11	Ephesians 3:14-21	*The power and riches of God*
JANUARY 12	Psalm 72:1-19	*Praise to God for the king*

The Baptism of Our Lord

SUNDAY	Isaiah 42:1-9	*The servant of the LORD brings justice*
	Psalm 29	*The voice of the LORD upon the waters*
	Acts 10:34-43	*Jesus' ministry after his baptism*
	Matthew 3:13-17	*Christ revealed as God's servant*
MONDAY	Genesis 35:1-15	*God calls and blesses Jacob*
TUESDAY	Jeremiah 1:4-10	*God calls Jeremiah*
WEDNESDAY	Matthew 12:15-21	*The words of Isaiah applied to Jesus*
THURSDAY	Isaiah 51:7-16	*God saves the people through water*
FRIDAY	Acts 8:4-13	*Philip preaches and baptizes*
SATURDAY	Psalm 89:5-37	*God anoints David to be a son*

Second Sunday after the Epiphany

SUNDAY	Isaiah 49:1-7	*The servant brings light to the nations*
	Psalm 40:1-11	*Doing the will of God*
	1 Corinthians 1:1-9	*Paul's greeting to the church at Corinth*
	John 1:29-42	*Christ revealed as the Lamb of God*
MONDAY	Exodus 12:1-13, 21-28	*The Passover lamb*
TUESDAY	Isaiah 53:1-12	*The one like a lamb*
WEDNESDAY	Matthew 9:14-17	*Christ, the bridegroom, the new wine*
THURSDAY	Isaiah 48:12-21	*God saves the people through water*
FRIDAY	Acts 8:26-40	*Philip teaches about the lamb*
SATURDAY	Psalm 40:6-17	*Not sacrifice, but divine mercy*

Third Sunday after the Epiphany

SUNDAY	Isaiah 9:1-4	*Light shines for those in darkness*
	Psalm 27:1, 4-9	*The LORD is light*
	1 Corinthians 1:10-18	*An appeal for unity in the gospel*
	Matthew 4:12-23	*Christ revealed as a prophet*
MONDAY	Judges 6:11-24	*God calls Gideon to lead the people*
TUESDAY	Judges 7:12-22	*God leads Gideon to victory*
WEDNESDAY	Luke 1:67-79	*Christ, the light dawning*
THURSDAY	Genesis 49:1-2, 8-13, 21-26	*Judah, Zebulum, Napthali blessed*
FRIDAY	Philippians 2:12-18	*Call to shine like stars*
SATURDAY	Psalm 27:7-14	*God, our light, our victory*

Fourth Sunday after the Epiphany

SUNDAY	Micah 6:1-8	*The offering of justice, kindness, humility*
	Psalm 15	*Abiding on the holy hill*
	1 Corinthians 1:18-31	*Christ crucified, the wisdom and power of God*
	Matthew 5:1-12	*The teaching of Christ: Beatitudes*
MONDAY	Ruth 1:1-18	*Ruth, one of the poor*
TUESDAY	Ruth 2:1-16	*Ruth, one of the hungry*
WEDNESDAY	Luke 6:17-26	*The beatitudes in Luke*
THURSDAY	Ruth 3:1-13; 4:13-22	*Ruth, one of the blessed*
FRIDAY	Philemon 1-25	*Concerning the slave Onesimus*
SATURDAY	Psalm 37:1-17	*God will bless the righteous*

Fifth Sunday after the Epiphany

SUNDAY	Isaiah 58:1-9a [9b-12]	*The fast God chooses*
	Psalm 112:1-9 [10]	*Light shines in the darkness*
	1 Corinthians 2:1-12 [13-16]	*God's wisdom revealed through the Spirit*
	Matthew 5:13-20	*The teaching of Christ: salt and light*
MONDAY	2 Kings 22:3-20	*Huldah urges Josiah to keep the law*
TUESDAY	2 Kings 23:1-8, 21-25	*King Josiah keeps the law*
WEDNESDAY	John 8:12-30	*You are the light of the world*
THURSDAY	Proverbs 6:6-23	*The law is a lamp*
FRIDAY	2 Corinthians 4:1-12	*Christ, the light*
SATURDAY	Psalm 119:105-112	*The law is light*

Sixth Sunday after the Epiphany

SUNDAY	Deuteronomy 30:15-20	*Choose life*
	or Sirach 15:15-20	*Choose between life and death*
	Psalm 119:1-8	*Happy are they who walk in the law*
	1 Corinthians 3:1-9	*God gives the growth*
	Matthew 5:21-37	*The teaching of Christ: forgiveness*
MONDAY	Exodus 20:1-21	*The Ten Commandments*
TUESDAY	Deuteronomy 23:21—24:4, 10-15	*Israelite communal laws*
WEDNESDAY	Matthew 19:1-12	*Jesus teaches about divorce*
THURSDAY	Proverbs 2:1-15	*The way of wisdom*
FRIDAY	James 2:1-13	*The law, judgment, and mercy*
SATURDAY	Psalm 119:9-16	*I delight in the law*

Seventh Sunday after the Epiphany

SUNDAY	Leviticus 19:1-2, 9-18	*Acts of mercy and justice*
	Psalm 119:33-40	*Walking in the path of the law*
	1 Corinthians 3:10-11, 16-23	*Allegiance to Christ, not human leaders*
	Matthew 5:38-48	*The teaching of Christ: love*
MONDAY	Leviticus 24:10-23	*An eye for an eye*
TUESDAY	Proverbs 25:11-22	*Caring for the enemy*
WEDNESDAY	Matthew 7:1-12	*The golden rule*
THURSDAY	Genesis 31:1-7, 17-26, 44-50	*Laban and Jacob reconcile*
FRIDAY	Romans 12:9-21	*Caring for the enemy*
SATURDAY	Psalm 119:57-64	*Keeping the law in spite of the wicked*

Eighth Sunday after the Epiphany

SUNDAY	Isaiah 49:8-16a	*God's motherly compassion*
	Psalm 131	*A child upon its mother's breast*
	1 Corinthians 4:1-5	*Servants accountable to God*
	Matthew 6:24-34	*The teaching of Christ: trust in God*
MONDAY	Deuteronomy 32:1-14	*God's care for the chosen people*
TUESDAY	1 Kings 17:1-16	*God feeds the widow*
WEDNESDAY	Luke 12:22-31	*Do not worry*
THURSDAY	Isaiah 66:7-13	*God as a nursing mother*
FRIDAY	1 Corinthians 4:6-21	*The life of an apostle*
SATURDAY	Psalm 104:10-28	*God cares for all the earth*

The Transfiguration of Our Lord

SUNDAY	Exodus 24:12-18	*Moses enters the cloud of God's glory*
	Psalm 2	*The one begotten of God*
	2 Peter 1:16-21	*Shining with the glory of God*
	Matthew 17:1-9	*Christ revealed as God's beloved Son*
MONDAY	Exodus 33:7-23	*Moses sees God*
TUESDAY	1 Kings 19:1-3, 9-18	*Elijah hears God*

Lent

Ash Wednesday

	Joel 2:1-2, 12-17	*Return to God*
	or Isaiah 58:1-12	*The fast that God chooses*
	Psalm 51:1-17	*Plea for mercy*
	2 Corinthians 5:20b—6:10	*Now is the day of salvation*
	Matthew 6:1-6, 16-21	*The practice of faith*
THURSDAY	Jonah 3:1-10	*Nineveh repents*
FRIDAY	Jonah 4:1-11	*Jonah is reproved*
SATURDAY	Isaiah 58:1-12	*God calls for our repentance*

First Sunday in Lent

SUNDAY	Genesis 2:15-17; 3:1-7	*Eating of the tree of knowledge*
	Psalm 32	*Mercy embraces us*
	Romans 5:12-19	*Death came, life comes*
	Matthew 4:1-11	*The temptation of Jesus*
MONDAY	Genesis 4:1-16	*God protects Cain, the murderer*
TUESDAY	Exodus 34:1-9, 27-28	*God's revelation of mercy*
WEDNESDAY	Matthew 18:6-14	*Temptation and forgiveness*
THURSDAY	1 Kings 19:1-8	*An angel feeds Elijah in the wilderness*
FRIDAY	Hebrews 4:14—5:14	*Christ was tempted*
SATURDAY	Psalm 38	*Confessing our sin*

Second Sunday in Lent

SUNDAY	Genesis 12:1-4a	*The blessing of God upon Abram*
	Psalm 121	*The LORD who watches over you*
	Romans 4:1-5, 13-17	*The promise to those of Abraham's faith*
	John 3:1-17	*The mission of Christ: saving the world*
MONDAY	Isaiah 65:17-25	*God promises a new creation*
TUESDAY	Ezekiel 36:22-32	*God will renew the people*
WEDNESDAY	John 8:1-11	*Jesus does not condemn the sinner*
THURSDAY	Numbers 21:4-9	*Moses lifts up the serpent*
FRIDAY	Romans 4:6-13	*Abraham saved through faith*
SATURDAY	Psalm 128	*God promises life*

Third Sunday in Lent

SUNDAY	Exodus 17:1-7	*Water from the rock*
	Psalm 95	*The rock of our salvation*
	Romans 5:1-11	*Reconciled to God by Christ's death*
	John 4:5-42	*The woman at the well*
MONDAY	Genesis 24:1-27	*Rebekah at the well*
TUESDAY	Genesis 29:1-14	*Rachel at the well*
WEDNESDAY	John 7:14-31, 37-39	*Drink of Jesus, the Messiah*
THURSDAY	Jeremiah 2:4-13	*God, the living water*
FRIDAY	2 John 1-13	*A woman reminded to abide in Christ*
SATURDAY	Psalm 81	*We drink from the rock*

Fourth Sunday in Lent

SUNDAY	1 Samuel 16:1-13	*David is chosen and anointed*
	Psalm 23	*My head anointed with oil*
	Ephesians 5:8-14	*Live as children of light*
	John 9:1-41	*The man born blind*
MONDAY	Isaiah 59:9-19	*We are blind and await God*
TUESDAY	Isaiah 42:14-21	*God will heal the blind*
WEDNESDAY	Matthew 9:27-34	*Jesus heals the blind*
THURSDAY	Isaiah 60:17-22	*God our light*
FRIDAY	Acts 9:1-20	*Saul's blindness*
SATURDAY	Psalm 146:3-9	*Praise to God*

Fifth Sunday in Lent

SUNDAY	Ezekiel 37:1-14	*The dry bones of Israel*
	Psalm 130	*Mercy and redemption*
	Romans 8:6-11	*Life in the Spirit*
	John 11:1-45	*The raising of Lazarus*
MONDAY	1 Kings 17:17-24	*Elijah raises the widow's son*
TUESDAY	2 Kings 4:18-37	*Elisha raises the Shumenite child*
WEDNESDAY	Matthew 22:23-33	*God of the living*
THURSDAY	Jeremiah 32:1-9, 36-41	*Jeremiah buys a field*
FRIDAY	Ephesians 2:1-10	*Alive in Christ*
SATURDAY	Psalm 143	*Save me from death*

Sunday of the Passion

PALM SUNDAY	Matthew 21:1-11	*Jesus enters Jerusalem*
	Psalm 118: 1-2, 19-29	*Open the gates*
	Isaiah 50:4-9a	*The servant submits to suffering*
	Psalm 31:9-16	*I commend my spirit*
	Philippians 2:5-11	*Death on a cross*
	Matthew 26:14—27:66	*The passion and death of Jesus*
MONDAY	John 12:1-11	*Mary of Bethany anoints Jesus*
TUESDAY	John 12:20-36	*Jesus speaks of his death*
WEDNESDAY	John 13:21-32	*Jesus foretells his betrayal*

The Three Days

Maundy Thursday

Exodus 12:1-4 [5-10] 11-14	*The passover of the LORD*
Psalm 116:1-2, 12-19	*The cup of salvation*
1 Corinthians 11:23-26	*Proclaim the Lord's death until he comes*
John 13:1-17, 31b-35	*The service of Christ: footwashing and meal*

Good Friday

Isaiah 52:13—53:12	*The suffering servant*
Psalm 22	*Why have you forsaken me?*
Hebrews 10:16-25	*The way to God is opened*
or Hebrews 4:14-16; 5:7-9	*Jesus, the merciful high priest*
John 18:1—19:42	*The passion and death of Jesus*

Holy Saturday

| Job 14:1-14 | *Hope for a tree* |

11

The Resurrection of Our Lord | Vigil of Easter

READINGS AND RESPONSES	Genesis 1:1—2:4a	*Creation*
	Psalm 136:1-9, 23-36	*God's mercy endures forever*
	Genesis 7:1-5, 11-18; 8:6-18; 9:8-13	*The flood*
	Psalm 46	*The God of Jacob is our stronghold*
	Genesis 22:1-18	*The testing of Abraham*
	Psalm 16	*You will show me the path of life*
	Exodus 14:10-31; 15:20-21	*Israel's deliverance at the Red Sea*
	Exodus 15:1b-13, 17-18	*The LORD has triumphed gloriously*
	Isaiah 55:1-11	*Salvation freely offered to all*
	Isaiah 12:2-6	*The wells of salvation*
	Proverbs 8:1-8, 19-21; 9:4b-6	
	or Baruch 3:9-15, 32—4:4	*The wisdom of God*
	Psalm 19	*The law is just*
	Ezekiel 36:24-28	*A new heart and a new spirit*
	Psalm 42 and Psalm 43	*My soul thirsts for the living God*
	Ezekiel 37:1-14	*The valley of the dry bones*
	Psalm 143	*Revive me, O LORD*
	Zephaniah 3:14-20	*The gathering of God's people*
	Psalm 98	*Lift up your voice, rejoice and sing*
	Jonah 3:1-10	*The call of Jonah*
	Jonah 2:1-3 [4-6] 7-9	*Deliverance belongs to our God*
	Deuteronomy 31:19-30	*The song of Moses*
	Deuteronomy 32:1-4, 7, 36a, 43a	*Justice for the people*
	Daniel 3:1-29	*The fiery furnace*
	Song of the Three Young Men 3:35-65	*Sing praise to the LORD*
	Romans 6:3-11	*Dying and rising with Christ*
	Psalm 114	*Tremble, O earth*
	Matthew 28:1-10	*Proclaim the resurrection*

Easter

The Resurrection of Our Lord | Easter Day

SUNDAY	Acts 10:34-43	*God raised Jesus on the third day*
	or Jeremiah 31:1-6	*Joy at the restoration of God's people*
	Psalm 118:1-2, 14-24	*On this day the LORD has acted*
	Colossians 3:1-4	*Raised with Christ*
	or Acts 10:34-43	*God raised Jesus on the third day*
	John 20:1-18	*Seeing the risen Christ*
	or Matthew 28:1-10	*Proclaim the resurrection*

The Resurrection of Our Lord | Easter Evening

SUNDAY	Isaiah 25:6-9	*The feast of victory*
	Psalm 114	*Hallelujah*
	1 Corinthians 5:6b-8	*Celebrating with sincerity and truth*
	Luke 24:13-49	*At evening, the risen Christ is revealed*
MONDAY	Exodus 14:10-31; 15:20-21	*Israel crosses over the Sea*
TUESDAY	Joshua 3:1-17	*Israel crosses into the promised land*
WEDNESDAY	Matthew 28:1-10	*Matthew's account of the resurrection*
THURSDAY	Song of Solomon 2:3-15	*The song of lovers in the garden*
FRIDAY	Colossians 3:1-17	*The new life in Christ*
SATURDAY	Exodus 15:1-18	*The song of the sea*

Second Sunday of Easter

SUNDAY	Acts 2:14a, 22-32	*God fulfills the promise to David*
	Psalm 16	*Fullness of joy*
	1 Peter 1:3-9	*New birth to a living hope*
	John 20:19-31	*Beholding the wounds of the risen Christ*
MONDAY	Jonah 1:1-17	*Jonah saved from the sea*
TUESDAY	Jonah 2:1-10	*Jonah's praise for deliverance*
WEDNESDAY	Matthew 12:38-42	*Jesus speaks of the sign of Jonah*
THURSDAY	Judges 6:36-40	*Gideon and the sign of the fleece*
FRIDAY	1 Corinthians 15:12-28	*Paul teaches the resurrection*
SATURDAY	Psalm 114	*God saves through water*

Third Sunday of Easter

SUNDAY	Acts 2:14a, 36-41	*Receiving God's promise through baptism*
	Psalm 116:1-4, 12-19	*I will call upon God*
	1 Peter 1:17-23	*Born anew*
	Luke 24:13-35	*Eating with the risen Christ*
MONDAY	Genesis 18:1-14	*Abraham and Sarah eat with God*
TUESDAY	Exodus 24:1-11	*Moses and the elders eat with God*
WEDNESDAY	John 21:1-14	*Jesus eats with the disciples*
THURSDAY	Proverbs 8:32—9:6	*Wisdom serves a meal*
FRIDAY	1 Peter 1:8-16	*A holy life*
SATURDAY	Psalm 134	*Praise to God*

Fourth Sunday of Easter

SUNDAY	Acts 2:42-47	*The believers' common life*
	Psalm 23	*The LORD is my shepherd*
	1 Peter 2:19-25	*Follow the shepherd, even in suffering*
	John 10:1-10	*Christ, the shepherd*
MONDAY	Ezekiel 34:1-16	*God, the true shepherd*
TUESDAY	Ezekiel 34:23-31	*God will provide perfect pasture*
WEDNESDAY	Matthew 20:17-28	*Jesus came to serve*
THURSDAY	Jeremiah 23:1-8	*God will gather the flock*
FRIDAY	1 Peter 2:9-17	*Live as God's people*
SATURDAY	Psalm 23	*God, our shepherd*

Fifth Sunday of Easter

SUNDAY	Acts 7:55-60	*The martyrdom of Stephen*
	Psalm 31:1-5, 15-16	*I commend my spirit*
	1 Peter 2:2-10	*God's chosen people*
	John 14:1-14	*Christ, the way, truth, and life*
MONDAY	Exodus 13:17-22	*God leads the way*
TUESDAY	Proverbs 3:5-18	*God, the truth and life*
WEDNESDAY	John 8:31-38	*Jesus, the truth of God*
THURSDAY	Acts 6:8-15	*Stephen is arrested*
FRIDAY	Acts 7:44-60	*Stephen's martyrdom*
SATURDAY	Psalm 102:1-17	*Prayer for deliverance*

Sixth Sunday of Easter

SUNDAY	Acts 17:22-31	*Paul's message to the Athenians*
	Psalm 66:8-20	*Be joyful in God, all you lands*
	1 Peter 3:13-22	*The days of Noah, a sign of baptism*
	John 14:15-21	*Christ our advocate*
MONDAY	Deuteronomy 5:22-33	*Moses delivers God's commandments*
TUESDAY	Deuteronomy 31:1-13	*Moses promises God's presence*
WEDNESDAY	Acts 17:32—18:11	*God promises to be with Paul*

The Ascension of Our Lord

	Acts 1:1-11	*Jesus sends the apostles*
	Psalm 47	*God has gone up with a shout*
	or Psalm 93	*God's throne has been established*
	Ephesians 1:15-23	*Seeing the risen and ascended Christ*
	Luke 24:44-53	*Christ present in all times and places*
FRIDAY	John 8:21-30	*Jesus speaks of going to the Father*
SATURDAY	Psalm 93	*Praise to God who reigns*

Seventh Sunday of Easter

SUNDAY	Acts 1:6-14	*Jesus' companions at prayer*
	Psalm 68:1-10, 32-35	*Sing to God*
	1 Peter 4:12-14; 5:6-11	*God sustains those who suffer*
	John 17:1-11	*Christ's prayer for his disciples*
MONDAY	Leviticus 9:1-11, 22-24	*High priest Aaron offers sacrifice*
TUESDAY	1 Kings 8:54-65	*King Solomon offers sacrifice*
WEDNESDAY	John 3:31-36	*The Son and the Father*
THURSDAY	Numbers 16:41-50	*The high priest Aaron makes atonement*
FRIDAY	1 Peter 3:21—4:11	*The baptized life*
SATURDAY	Psalm 99	*The priests and people praise God*

Vigil of Pentecost

	Exodus 19:1-9	*The covenant at Sinai*
	or Acts 2:1-11	*Filled with the Spirit*
	Psalm 33:12-22	*Our help and our shield*
	or Psalm 130	*There is forgiveness*
	Romans 8:14-17, 22-27	*Praying with the Spirit*
	John 7:37-39	*Jesus, the true living water*

The Day of Pentecost

SUNDAY	Acts 2:1-21	*Filled with the Spirit*
	or Numbers 11:24-30	*The spirit and the elders of Israel*
	Psalm 104:24-34, 35b	*Renewing the face of the earth*
	1 Corinthians 12:3b-13	*Varieties of gifts from the same Spirit*
	or Acts 2:1-21	*Filled with the Spirit*
	John 20:19-23	*The Spirit poured out*
	or John 7:37-39	*Jesus, the true living water*
MONDAY	Joel 2:18-29	*God promises the spirit*
TUESDAY	Ezekiel 39:7-8, 21-29	*God promises the spirit*
WEDNESDAY	John 7:37-39	*The coming of the Holy Spirit*
THURSDAY	Numbers 11:24-30	*All the elders receive the spirit*
FRIDAY	Romans 8:14-27	*The life of the Holy Spirit*
SATURDAY	Psalm 104:1-9, 24-35	*God's spirit throughout the earth*

The Holy Trinity

SUNDAY	Genesis 1:1—2:4a	*The creation of the heavens and the earth*
	Psalm 8	*How exalted is your name*
	2 Corinthians 13:11-13	*Paul's farewell*
	Matthew 28:16-20	*Living in the community of the Trinity*
MONDAY	Job 38:1-21	*The creation story from Job*
TUESDAY	Job 38:34—39:4, 26—40:5	*More of Job's creation story*
WEDNESDAY	John 14:15-31	*The Father, the Son, the Spirit*
THURSDAY	1 Kings 8:10-13, 22-30	*Solomon's prayer to God*
FRIDAY	1 Corinthians 12:1-13	*The Spirit in the community*
SATURDAY	Psalm 29	*Praise the glory of God*

Sunday between May 24 and 28 inclusive (Proper 3)

Isaiah 49:8-16a	*God's motherly compassion*
Psalm 131	*A child upon its mother's breast*
1 Corinthians 4:1-5	*Servants accountable to God*
Matthew 6:24-34	*The teaching of Christ: trust in God*

Sunday between May 29 and June 4 inclusive (Proper 4)

SUNDAY	Deuteronomy 11:18-21, 26-28	*Keeping the words of God*
	Psalm 31:1-5, 19-24	*I commend my spirit*
	or Genesis 6:9-22; 7:24; 8:14-19	*The great flood*
	Psalm 46	*The God of Jacob is our stronghold*
	Romans 1:16-17; 3:22b-28 [29-31]	*Justified by God's grace as a gift*
	Matthew 7:21-29	*The teaching of Christ: doing the works of God*
MONDAY	Joshua 8:30-35	*Joshua renews the Mosaic covenant*
TUESDAY	Joshua 24:1-2, 11-28	*The Israelites renew the covenant*
WEDNESDAY	Matthew 7:13-20	*The narrow gate*
THURSDAY	Job 28:12-28	*The way of wisdom*
FRIDAY	Romans 3:9-22a	*All have sinned*
SATURDAY	Psalm 52	*The wicked and the righteous*

Sunday between June 5 and 11 inclusive (Proper 5)

SUNDAY	Hosea 5:15—6:6	*God desires steadfast love*
	Psalm 50:7-15	*The salvation of God*
	or Genesis 12:1-9	*Abram's journey in the promise*
	Psalm 33:1-12	*Happy is the nation whose God is the LORD*
	Romans 4:13-25	*The promise to those of Abraham's faith*
	Matthew 9:9-13, 18-26	*Christ heals a woman and raises a girl*
MONDAY	Hosea 8:11-14; 10:1-2	*God rejects Israel's sacrifices*
TUESDAY	Hosea 14:1-9	*God will be merciful to Israel*
WEDNESDAY	Matthew 12:1-8	*Mercy, not sacrifice*
THURSDAY	Leviticus 15:25-31; 22:1-9	*Those bleeding or dead are impure*
FRIDAY	Hebrews 13:1-16	*Sacrifices pleasing to God*
SATURDAY	Psalm 40:1-8	*God's will, not sacrifice*

Sunday between June 12 and 18 inclusive (Proper 6)

SUNDAY	Exodus 19:2-8a	*The covenant with Israel at Sinai*
	Psalm 100	*We are God's people*
	or Genesis 18:1-15 [21:1-7]	*God appears to Abraham and Sarah*
	Psalm 116:1, 10-17	*I will call upon the name of the LORD*
	Romans 5:1-8	*While we were sinners, Christ died for us*
	Matthew 9:35-10:8 [9-23]	*The sending of the Twelve*
MONDAY	Joshua 1:1-11	*God calls Joshua*
TUESDAY	1 Samuel 3:1-19	*God calls Samuel*
WEDNESDAY	Luke 6:12-19	*Jesus chooses the apostles*
THURSDAY	Proverbs 4:10-27	*Choosing the way of wisdom*
FRIDAY	2 Thessalonians 2:13—3:5	*The life of those chosen by God*
SATURDAY	Psalm 105:1-11, 37-45	*God saves the chosen people*

Sunday between June 19 and 25 inclusive (Proper 7)

SUNDAY	Jeremiah 20:7-13	*The prophet must speak*
	Psalm 69:7-10 [11-15] 16-18	*Draw near to me*
	or Genesis 21:8-21	*The rescue of Hagar and Ishmael*
	Psalm 86:1-10, 16-17	*Have mercy upon me*
	Romans 6:1b-11	*Buried and raised with Christ in baptism*
	Matthew 10:24-39	*The cost of discipleship*
MONDAY	Jeremiah 26:1-12	*Jeremiah prophesies against Jerusalem*
TUESDAY	Jeremiah 38:1-13	*Jeremiah imprisoned and released*
WEDNESDAY	Matthew 10:5-23	*Jesus speaks about persecutions*
THURSDAY	Micah 7:1-7	*The corruption of the people*
FRIDAY	Revelation 2:1-11	*Enduring patiently*
SATURDAY	Psalm 6	*Prayer for deliverance*

Sunday between June 26 and July 2 inclusive (Proper 8)

SUNDAY	Jeremiah 28:5-9	*The test of a true prophet*
	Psalm 89:1-4, 15-18	*I sing of your love*
	or Genesis 22:1-14	*The testing of Abraham*
	Psalm 13	*Give light to my eyes*
	Romans 6:12-23	*No longer under law but under grace*
	Matthew 10:40-42	*Welcome Christ in those he sends*
MONDAY	1 Kings 21:1-16	*Ahab and Jezebel sin against Naboth*
TUESDAY	1 Kings 21:17-29	*The prophet Elijah confronts Ahab*
WEDNESDAY	Matthew 11:16-24	*Jesus prophecies against the city*
THURSDAY	Jeremiah 18:1-11	*Jeremiah at the potter's wheel*
FRIDAY	1 John 4:1-6	*Testing the spirits*
SATURDAY	Psalm 119:161-168	*Loving God's law*

Sunday between July 3 and 9 inclusive (Proper 9)

SUNDAY	Zechariah 9:9-12	*The king comes in peace*
	Psalm 145:8-14	*The LORD is gracious and full of compassion*
	or Genesis 24:34-38, 42-49, 58-67	*The marriage of Isaac and Rebekah*
	Psalm 45:10-17	*God has anointed you*
	or Song of Solomon 2:8-13	*Arise, my love and come away*
	Romans 7:15-25a	*The struggle within the self*
	Matthew 11:16-19, 25-30	*The yoke of discipleship*
MONDAY	Jeremiah 27:1-11, 16-22	*Jeremiah wears the evil yoke*
TUESDAY	Jeremiah 28:10-17	*Hananiah breaks Jeremiah's yoke and dies*
WEDNESDAY	John 13:1-17	*Jesus washes the disciples' feet*
THURSDAY	Jeremiah 13:1-11	*Jeremiah's loincloth*
FRIDAY	Romans 7:1-20	*The law and sin*
SATURDAY	Psalm 131	*I rest like a weaned child on God*

Sunday between July 10 and 16 inclusive (Proper 10)

SUNDAY	Isaiah 55:10-13	*The growth of the word*
	Psalm 65:[1-8] 9-13	*Your paths overflow with plenty*
	or Genesis 25:19-34	*Esau sells his birthright to Jacob*
	Psalm 119:105-112	*Your word is a lantern to my feet*
	Romans 8:1-11	*Living according to the Spirit*
	Matthew 13:1-9, 18-23	*The parable of the sower and the seed*
MONDAY	Leviticus 26:3-20	*A rich and a poor harvest from God*
TUESDAY	Deuteronomy 28:1-14	*The blessings of obedience*
WEDNESDAY	Matthew 13:10-17	*The purpose of parables*
THURSDAY	Proverbs 11:23-30	*The fruit of righteousness*
FRIDAY	Ephesians 4:17—5:2	*The old life, the new life*
SATURDAY	Psalm 92	*The wicked as grass, the righteous a tree*

Sunday between July 17 and 23 inclusive (Proper 11)

SUNDAY	Isaiah 44:6-8	*There is no other God than the* LORD
	or Wisdom 12:13, 16-19	*God's sovereignty*
	Psalm 86:11-17	*Teach me your way, O* LORD
	or Genesis 28:10-19a	*Jacob's dream of the ladder from heaven*
	Psalm 139:1-12, 23-24	*You have searched me out and known me*
	Romans 8:12-25	*The revealing of the children of God*
	Matthew 13:24-30, 36-43	*The parable of the weeds*
MONDAY	Nahum 1:1-13	*The wrath and the mercy of God*
TUESDAY	Zephaniah 3:1-13	*The wicked convert to God*
WEDNESDAY	Revelation 14:12-20	*The harvest at the end of time*
THURSDAY	Daniel 12:1-13	*The righteous will shine*
FRIDAY	Galatians 4:21—5:1	*An allegory about those saved*
SATURDAY	Psalm 75	*God's judgment*

Sunday between July 24 and 30 inclusive (Proper 12)

SUNDAY	1 Kings 3:5-12	*Solomon's prayer for wisdom*
	Psalm 119:129-136	*Your word gives light and understanding*
	or Genesis 29:15-28	*Leah and Rachel become Jacob's wives*
	Psalm 105:1-11, 45b	*God's promises to Jacob*
	or Psalm 128	*Happy are they who follow in God's ways*
	Romans 8:26-39	*Nothing can separate us from God's love*
	Matthew 13:31-33, 44-52	*Parables of the reign of heaven*
MONDAY	1 Kings 3:16-28	*Solomon's wisdom in judgment*
TUESDAY	1 Kings 4:29-34	*God gave Solomon wisdom*
WEDNESDAY	Mark 4:30-34	*Jesus' use of parables*
THURSDAY	Proverbs 1:1-7, 20-33	*The call of wisdom*
FRIDAY	Ephesians 6:10-18	*The allegory of the armor*
SATURDAY	Psalm 119:121-128	*Give me understanding*

Sunday between July 31 and August 6 inclusive (Proper 13)

SUNDAY	Isaiah 55:1-5	*Eat and drink that which truly satisfies*
	Psalm 145:8-9, 14-21	*You open wide your hand*
	or Genesis 32:22-31	*Jacob receives a blessing from God*
	Psalm 17:1-7, 15	*I shall see your face*
	Romans 9:1-5	*The glory of God's people in Israel*
	Matthew 14:13-21	*Jesus feeds 5000*
MONDAY	Deuteronomy 8:1-10	*God will feed the people*
TUESDAY	Deuteronomy 26:1-15	*A tithe from God's harvest*
WEDNESDAY	Matthew 15:32-39	*Jesus feeds 5000*
THURSDAY	Exodus 16:2-15, 31-35	*God feeds the people manna*
FRIDAY	Acts 2:37-47	*The believers breaking bread*
SATURDAY	Psalm 78:1-8, 17-29	*God fed the people manna*

Sunday between August 7 and 13 inclusive (Proper 14)

SUNDAY	1 Kings 19:9-18	*Elijah on Mount Horeb*
	Psalm 85:8-13	*I will listen*
	or Genesis 37:1-4, 12-28	*Joseph sold by his brothers*
	Psalm 105:1-6, 16-22, 45b	*Remembering Joseph*
	Romans 10:5-15	*The word of faith*
	Matthew 14:22-33	*Jesus walking on the sea*
MONDAY	Genesis 7:11—8:5	*God saves Noah from the flood*
TUESDAY	Genesis 19:15-29	*God saves Lot from Sodom and Gomorrah*
WEDNESDAY	Matthew 8:23-27	*Jesus stills the storm*
THURSDAY	Job 36:24-33; 37:14-24	*The waters of God's creation*
FRIDAY	Romans 9:14-29	*God's wrath, God's mercy*
SATURDAY	Psalm 18:1-19	*God saves me from the waters*

Sunday between August 14 and 20 inclusive (Proper 15)

SUNDAY	Isaiah 56:1, 6-8	*A house of prayer for all peoples*
	Psalm 67	*Let all the peoples praise God*
	or Genesis 45:1-15	*Joseph reconciles with his brothers*
	Psalm 133	*How good it is to live in unity*
	Romans 11:1-2a, 29-32	*God's mercy to all, Jew and Gentile*
	Matthew 15:[10-20] 21-28	*The Canaanite woman's daughter is healed*
MONDAY	2 Kings 5:1-14	*The foreigner Naaman is healed*
TUESDAY	Isaiah 66:18-23	*All nations shall come to worship*
WEDNESDAY	Matthew 8:1-13	*Jesus heals many people*
THURSDAY	Acts 15:1-21	*The believing Jews accept the Gentiles*
FRIDAY	Romans 11:13-29	*God saves Jews and Gentiles*
SATURDAY	Psalm 87	*Foreigners praising God in Zion*

Sunday between August 21 and 27 inclusive (Proper 16)

SUNDAY	Isaiah 51:1-6	*God's enduring salvation*
	Psalm 138	*O LORD, your love endures forever*
	or Exodus 1:8—2:10	*Pharaoh's daughter takes Moses as her son*
	Psalm 124	*We have escaped like a bird*
	Romans 12:1-8	*One body in Christ, with gifts that differ*
	Matthew 16:13-20	*The profession of Peter's faith*
MONDAY	1 Samuel 7:3-13	*Samuel raises the Ebenezer stone*
TUESDAY	Deuteronomy 32:18-20, 28-39	*Praise the rock that is God*
WEDNESDAY	Matthew 26:6-13	*A woman anoints Jesus with oil*
THURSDAY	Isaiah 28:14-22	*God lays a cornerstone in Zion*
FRIDAY	Romans 9:30—10:4	*Christ the stumbling stone*
SATURDAY	Psalm 18:1-3, 20-32	*God the Rock*

Sunday between Aug. 28 and Sept. 3 inclusive (Proper 17)

SUNDAY	Jeremiah 15:15-21	*God fortifies the prophet*
	Psalm 26:1-8	*Your love is before my eyes*
	or Exodus 3:1-15	*From the blazing bush God calls Moses*
	Psalm 105:1-6, 23-26, 45c	*Remembering Moses*
	Romans 12:9-21	*Live in harmony*
	Matthew 16:21-28	*The rebuke to Peter*
MONDAY	2 Samuel 11:2-26	*David sins*
TUESDAY	2 Samuel 11:27b—12:15	*Nathan rebukes David*
WEDNESDAY	Matthew 12:22-32	*Jesus comes to cast out Satan*
THURSDAY	Jeremiah 17:5-18	*The vindication of the righteous*
FRIDAY	Revelation 3:1-13	*Rewarding those with endurance*
SATURDAY	Psalm 17	*The righteous shall see God*

Sunday between September 4 and 10 inclusive (Proper 18)

SUNDAY	Ezekiel 33:7-11	*The prophet's responsibility*
	Psalm 119:33-40	*The path of your commandments*
	or Exodus 12:1-14	*The passover*
	Psalm 149	*Sing praise in the congregation*
	Romans 13:8-14	*Live honorably as in the day*
	Matthew 18:15-20	*Reconciliation in the community of faith*
MONDAY	Leviticus 4:27-31; 5:14-16	*Atoning for sin in the community*
TUESDAY	Deuteronomy 17:2-13	*Punishment for sin in the community*
WEDNESDAY	Matthew 21:18-22	*Jesus teaches about communal prayer*
THURSDAY	Leviticus 16:1-5, 20-28	*The scapegoat cleanses the community*
FRIDAY	Romans 13:1-7	*Obeying authority*
SATURDAY	Psalm 119:65-72	*The law humbles me*

Sunday between September 11 and 17 inclusive (Proper 19)

SUNDAY	Genesis 50:15-21	*Joseph reconciles with his brothers*
	Psalm 103:[1-7] 8-13	*The LORD is full of compassion and mercy*
	or Exodus 14:19-31	*Israel's deliverance at the Red Sea*
	Psalm 114	*Tremble, O earth*
	or Exodus 15:1b-11, 20-21	*The LORD triumphed gloriously*
	Romans 14:1-12	*Diversity in the community of faith*
	Matthew 18:21-35	*A parable of forgiveness*
MONDAY	Genesis 37:12-36	*Joseph's brothers sin against him*
TUESDAY	Genesis 41:53—42:17	*Joseph acts harshly against them*
WEDNESDAY	Matthew 6:7-15	*Forgiving one another*
THURSDAY	Genesis 45:1-20	*Joseph forgives his brothers*
FRIDAY	Romans 14:13—15:2	*Building each other up*
SATURDAY	Psalm 133	*How good it is to live in unity*

Sunday between September 18 and 24 inclusive (Proper 20)

SUNDAY	Jonah 3:10—4:11	*God's concern for Nineveh*
	Psalm 145:1-8	*The LORD is slow to anger*
	or Exodus 16:2-15	*Manna and quails in the wilderness*
	Psalm 105:1-6, 37-45	*Remembering the wilderness*
	Philippians 1:21-30	*Standing firm in the gospel*
	Matthew 20:1-16	*The parable of the vineyard workers*
MONDAY	Genesis 27:1-29	*The younger son gets the blessing*
TUESDAY	Genesis 28:10-17	*God blesses the runaway Jacob*
WEDNESDAY	Matthew 19:23-30	*The last will be first*
THURSDAY	Isaiah 41:1-13	*God will be with the last*
FRIDAY	Romans 16:1-20	*Workers in the church of Rome*
SATURDAY	Psalm 106:1-12	*God's mercy*

Sunday between Sept. 25 and Oct. 1 inclusive (Proper 21)

SUNDAY	Ezekiel 18:1-4, 25-32	*The fairness of God's way*
	Psalm 25:1-9	*God's compassion and love*
	or Exodus 17:1-7	*Water from the rock*
	Psalm 78:1-4, 12-16	*Recounting God's power*
	Philippians 2:1-13	*Christ humbled to the point of death*
	Matthew 21:23-32	*A parable of doing God's will*
MONDAY	Judges 16:1-22	*Samson asked about his strength*
TUESDAY	Judges 16:23-31	*Samson prays to do God's will*
WEDNESDAY	Matthew 9:2-8	*Jesus' authority*
THURSDAY	Joshua 4:1-10, 19-24	*Joshua leads the people God's way*
FRIDAY	Philippians 1:3-30	*Proclaiming Christ*
SATURDAY	Psalm 28	*Prayer to do God's will*

Sunday between October 2 and 8 inclusive (Proper 22)

SUNDAY	Isaiah 5:1-7	*The song of the vineyard*
	Psalm 80:7-15	*Look down from heaven, O God*
	or Exodus 20:1-4, 7-9, 12-20	*The commandments given at Sinai*
	Psalm 19	*The law is just and rejoices the heart*
	Philippians 3:4b-14	*Nothing surpasses knowing Christ*
	Matthew 21:33-46	*The parable of the vineyard owner's son*
MONDAY	Ezekiel 19:10-14	*A lament for Israel the vine*
TUESDAY	Isaiah 27:1-6	*God will save Israel the vine*
WEDNESDAY	John 7:40-52	*Some accept, others reject Christ*
THURSDAY	Song of Solomon 8:5-14	*A love song for the vineyard*
FRIDAY	1 Peter 2:4-10	*Christ, the cornerstone*
SATURDAY	Psalm 144	*Prayer for blessing*

Sunday between October 9 and 15 inclusive (Proper 23)

SUNDAY	Isaiah 25:1-9	*The feast of victory*
	Psalm 23	*You spread a table before me*
	or Exodus 32:1-14	*The Israelites forge a golden calf*
	Psalm 106:1-6, 19-23	*God's favor for the people*
	Philippians 4:1-9	*Rejoice in the Lord always*
	Matthew 22:1-14	*The parable of the unwelcome guest*
MONDAY	Exodus 19:7-20	*God meets Moses on the mountain*
TUESDAY	Amos 9:5-15	*God will restore Israel on the mountain*
WEDNESDAY	John 6:25-35	*God will feed the believer*
THURSDAY	Song of Solomon 7:10—8:4	*Love like rich fruit*
FRIDAY	Philippians 3:13—4:1	*Hold fast to Christ*
SATURDAY	Psalm 34	*Taste and see*

Sunday between October 16 and 22 inclusive (Proper 24)

SUNDAY	Isaiah 45:1-7	*An earthly ruler works God's will*
	Psalm 96:1-9 [10-13]	*Ascribe to the LORD honor and power*
	or Exodus 33:12-23	*The glory of God revealed to Moses*
	Psalm 99	*Proclaim the greatness of God*
	1 Thessalonians 1:1-10	*Thanksgiving for the church at Thessalonica*
	Matthew 22:15-22	*A teaching about the emperor and God*
MONDAY	Daniel 3:1-30	*Three men disobey King Nebuchadnezzar*
TUESDAY	Daniel 6:1-28	*Daniel disobeys King Darius*
WEDNESDAY	Matthew 17:22-27	*Jesus pays the temple tax*
THURSDAY	Deuteronomy 17:14-20	*The limitations on royal authority*
FRIDAY	Revelation 18:1-10, 19-20	*The fall of Babylon*
SATURDAY	Psalm 98	*God reigns*

Sunday between October 23 and 29 inclusive (Proper 25)

SUNDAY	Leviticus 19:1-2, 15-18	*Acts of justice*
	Psalm 1	*Their delight is in the law*
	or Deuteronomy 34:1-12	*The death of Moses*
	Psalm 90:1-6, 13-17	*Show your servants your works*
	1 Thessalonians 2:1-8	*The apostle's concern*
	Matthew 22:34-46	*Loving God and neighbor*
MONDAY	Deuteronomy 6:1-9, 20-25	*The great commandment*
TUESDAY	Deuteronomy 10:10-22	*Moses urges the people to obey*
WEDNESDAY	Matthew 19:16-22	*Keeping the commandments*
THURSDAY	Proverbs 16:1-20	*It is good to obey*
FRIDAY	James 2:8-26	*Faith without works is dead*
SATURDAY	Psalm 119:41-48	*I will keep God's law*

Sunday between Oct. 30 and Nov. 5 inclusive (Proper 26)

SUNDAY	Micah 3:5-12	*Judgment upon corrupt rulers*
	Psalm 43	*Send out your light and truth*
	or Joshua 3:7-17	*Israel crosses into the land of promise*
	Psalm 107:1-7, 33-37	*Thanks for a beautiful land*
	1 Thessalonians 2:9-13	*The apostle's teaching*
	Matthew 23:1-12	*Humble yourselves*
MONDAY	1 Samuel 2:27-36	*Hope for a better priesthood*
TUESDAY	Ezekiel 13:1-16	*False prophets condemned*
WEDNESDAY	Matthew 23:13-28	*Woe to the scribes and Pharisees*
THURSDAY	Malachi 1:6—2:9	*False and true priests*
FRIDAY	1 Thessalonians 2:13-20	*Words to the church*
SATURDAY	Psalm 5	*God blesses the righteous*

Sunday between November 6 and 12 inclusive (Proper 27)

SUNDAY	Amos 5:18-24	*Let justice roll down like waters*
	Psalm 70	*You are my helper and my deliverer*
	or Wisdom 6:12-16	*Wisdom makes herself known*
	Wisdom 6:17-20	*The beginning of wisdom*
	or Joshua 24:1-3a, 14-25	*Joshua calls Israel*
	Psalm 78:1-7	*The power of God*
	1 Thessalonians 4:13-18	*The promise of the resurrection*
	Matthew 25:1-13	*Wise and foolish bridesmaids*
MONDAY	Joel 1:1-14	*Call to repentance*
TUESDAY	Joel 3:9-21	*Promise of a glorious future*
WEDNESDAY	Matthew 24:1-14	*Jesus foretells the end*
THURSDAY	Amos 8:7-14	*God's promised judgment*
FRIDAY	1 Thessalonians 3:6-13	*Stand firm in faith*
SATURDAY	Psalm 63	*God as a rich feast*

Sunday between November 13 and 19 inclusive (Proper 28)

SUNDAY	Zephaniah 1:7, 12-18	*The day of the LORD*
	Psalm 90:1-8 [9-11] 12	*Number your days*
	or Judges 4:1-7	*The judgeship of Deborah*
	Psalm 123	*Our eyes look to you, O God*
	1 Thessalonians 5:1-11	*Be alert for the day of the Lord*
	Matthew 25:14-30	*Slaves entrusted with talents*
MONDAY	Zechariah 1:7-17	*A vision of God's judgment and mercy*
TUESDAY	Zechariah 2:1-5; 5:1-4	*Visions of mercy and judgment*
WEDNESDAY	Matthew 24:45-51	*Parable of the unfaithful slave*
THURSDAY	Job 16:1-21	*A lament about unjust punishment*
FRIDAY	1 Thessalonians 4:1-12; 5:12-18	*The Christian life*
SATURDAY	Psalm 9:1-14	*God's reward of the righteous*

Christ the King (Proper 29)

SUNDAY	Ezekiel 34:1-16, 20-24	*God will shepherd Israel*
	Psalm 95:1-7a	*We are the people of God's pasture*
	or Ezekiel 34:11-16, 20-24	*God will shepherd Israel*
	Psalm 100	*We are the sheep of God's pasture*
	Ephesians 1:15-23	*The reign of Christ*
	Matthew 25:31-46	*The separation of sheep and goats*
MONDAY	Esther 2:1-18	*Lowly Esther becomes queen*
TUESDAY	Esther 8:3-17	*Queen Esther saves her people*
WEDNESDAY	John 5:19-40	*The judgment of the Son*
THURSDAY	Ezekiel 33:7-20	*The righteous will live*
FRIDAY	Revelation 19:1-9	*Praise of God's judgments*
SATURDAY	Psalm 7	*God the righteous judge*

Cycle B

Cycle B

First Sunday in Advent

SUNDAY	Isaiah 64:1-9	*God will come with power and compassion*
	Psalm 80:1-7, 17-19	*We shall be saved*
	1 Corinthians 1:3-9	*Gifts of grace sustain us*
	Mark 13:24-37	*The coming of the Son of Man*
MONDAY	Zechariah 13:1-9	*On that day God will save us*
TUESDAY	Zechariah 14:1-9	*Promises concerning that day*
WEDNESDAY	Matthew 24:15-31	*Be ready for that day*
THURSDAY	Micah 2:1-13	*God will gather you all*
FRIDAY	1 Thessalonians 4:1-18	*A life pleasing to God till the end*
SATURDAY	Psalm 79	*Prayer for deliverance*

Second Sunday in Advent

SUNDAY	Isaiah 40:1-11	*God's coming to the exiles*
	Psalm 85:1-2, 8-13	*Righteousness and peace*
	2 Peter 3:8-15a	*Waiting for the day of God*
	Mark 1:1-8	*John appears from the wilderness*
MONDAY	Isaiah 26:7-15	*The way of the righteous is level*
TUESDAY	Isaiah 4:2-6	*God will wash Israel clean*
WEDNESDAY	Mark 11:27-33	*The authority behind John's ministry*
THURSDAY	Malachi 2:10—3:1	*The coming messenger*
FRIDAY	Acts 11:1-18	*John and Peter baptize*
SATURDAY	Psalm 27	*God's level path*

Third Sunday in Advent

SUNDAY	Isaiah 61:1-4, 8-11	*Righteousness and praise flourish like a garden*
	Psalm 126	*God does great things for us*
	or Luke 1:47-55	*The mighty one raises the lowly*
	1 Thessalonians 5:16-24	*Kept in faith until the coming of Christ*
	John 1:6-8, 19-28	*A witness to the light*
MONDAY	1 Kings 18:1-18	*Elijah condemns King Ahab*
TUESDAY	2 Kings 2:9-22	*Elisha receives Elijah's spirit*
WEDNESDAY	Mark 9:9-13	*Questions about Elijah*
THURSDAY	Malachi 3:16—4:6	*Elijah and the coming one*
FRIDAY	Acts 3:17—4:4	*Peter preaches about the prophets*
SATURDAY	Psalm 125	*Prayer for blessing*

Fourth Sunday in Advent

SUNDAY	2 Samuel 7:1-11, 16	*God's promise to David*
	Luke 1:47-55	*The Lord lifts up the lowly*
	or Psalm 89:1-4, 19-26	*I sing of your love*
	Romans 16:25-27	*The mystery revealed in Jesus Christ*
	Luke 1:26-38	*The angel appears to Mary*
MONDAY	1 Samuel 1:1-18	*Hannah is promised a child*
TUESDAY	1 Samuel 1:19-28	*Hannah presents Samuel to God*
WEDNESDAY	Mark 11:1-11	*Jesus enters Jerusalem*
THURSDAY	Judges 13:2-24	*Manoah's wife bears Samson*
FRIDAY	Hebrews 8:1-13	*The mediator replaces the sanctuary*
SATURDAY	1 Samuel 2:1-10	*Hannah's song*

Christmas

The Nativity of Our Lord | Christmas Eve

DECEMBER 24	Isaiah 9:2-7	*A child is born for us*
	Psalm 96	*Let the earth be glad*
	Titus 2:11-14	*The grace of God has appeared*
	Luke 2:1-14 [15-20]	*God with us*

The Nativity of Our Lord | Christmas Dawn

DECEMBER 25	Isaiah 62:6-12	*God comes to restore the people*
	Psalm 97	*Light springs up for the righteous*
	Titus 3:4-7	*Saved through water and the Spirit*
	Luke 2:[1-7] 8-20	*The birth of the Messiah revealed to shepherds*

The Nativity of Our Lord | Christmas Day

DECEMBER 25	Isaiah 52:7-10	*Heralds announce God's salvation*
	Psalm 98	*The victory of our God*
	Hebrews 1:1-4 [5-12]	*God has spoken by a son*
	John 1:1-14	*The Word became flesh*
DECEMBER 26	Luke 2:1-20	*The story of Jesus' birth*
DECEMBER 27	Isaiah 62:6-12	*Your salvation comes*
DECEMBER 28	Psalm 100	*God's steadfast love*
DECEMBER 29	Genesis 1:1—2:4a	*The first creation story*
DECEMBER 30	Psalm 136	*God's steadfast love*
DECEMBER 31	Titus 2:11—3:7	*The life of those newly born*

The Name of Jesus

JANUARY 1	Numbers 6:22-27	*The Aaronic blessing*
	Psalm 8	*How exalted is your name*
	Galatians 4:4-7	*We are no longer slaves*
	or Philippians 2:5-11	*God takes on human form*
	Luke 2:15-21	*The child is named Jesus*

First Sunday after Christmas

SUNDAY	Isaiah 61:10—62:3	*Clothed in garments of salvation*
	Psalm 148	*God's glory is spread over earth*
	Galatians 4:4-7	*Children and heirs of God*
	Luke 2:22-40	*The presentation of the child*

MONDAY	Leviticus 12:1-8	*Laws on purification after childbirth*
TUESDAY	Exodus 13:11-16	*Laws on dedication of the firstborn son*
WEDNESDAY	Matthew 12:46-50	*Jesus' true family*
THURSDAY	Isaiah 49:5-15	*God like a nursing mother*
FRIDAY	Acts 13:42-52	*A light to the Gentiles*
SATURDAY	Psalm 145:1-13	*One generation shall praise God to another*

Second Sunday after Christmas

Sunday	Jeremiah 31:7-14	*Joy as God's scattered flock gathers*
	Psalm 147:12-20	*Praising God in Zion*
	or Sirach 24:1-12	*Wisdom lives among God's people*
	Wisdom 10:15-21	*Praising the holy name*
	Ephesians 1:3-14	*The will of God made known in Christ*
	John 1:[1-9] 10-18	*God with us*

Epiphany

The Epiphany of Our Lord

JANUARY 6	Isaiah 60:1-6	*Nations come to the light*
	Psalm 72:1-7, 10-14	*All shall bow down*
	Ephesians 3:1-12	*The gospel's promise for all*
	Matthew 2:1-12	*Christ revealed to the nations*

JANUARY 7	Exodus 1:22—2:10	*God saves Moses from Pharaoh*
JANUARY 8	Exodus 2:11-25	*Moses escapes from Pharaoh again*
JANUARY 9	John 8:39-59	*Jesus' name: I AM*
JANUARY 10	Isaiah 45:8-17	*God greater than all human power*
JANUARY 11	Ephesians 2:11-22	*Being one in Christ*
JANUARY 12	Psalm 110	*God will shatter kings*

The Baptism of Our Lord

SUNDAY	Genesis 1:1-5	*God creates light*
	Psalm 29	*The voice of the LORD upon the waters*
	Acts 19:1-7	*Baptized in the name of Jesus*
	Mark 1:4-11	*Jesus revealed as God's servant*
MONDAY	Genesis 17:1-14, 23-27	*Circumcision a covenant sign*
TUESDAY	Exodus 30:22-38	*Anointing a sign of holiness*
WEDNESDAY	John 1:29-34	*John's account of Jesus' baptism*
THURSDAY	Isaiah 41:14-20	*God gives water in the desert*
FRIDAY	Acts 22:2-16	*Paul describes his own baptism*
SATURDAY	Psalm 69:1-5, 30-36	*God will save through water*

Second Sunday after the Epiphany

SUNDAY	1 Samuel 3:1-10 [11-20]	*The calling of Samuel*
	Psalm 139:1-6, 13-18	*You have searched me out*
	1 Corinthians 6:12-20	*Glorify God in your body*
	John 1:43-51	*The calling of the first disciples*
MONDAY	1 Samuel 9:27—10:8	*Samuel anoints Saul king*
TUESDAY	1 Samuel 15:10-31	*Samuel rebukes King Saul*
WEDNESDAY	Luke 18:15-17	*Jesus blesses little children*
THURSDAY	Genesis 16:1-14	*Hagar sees God and is blessed*
FRIDAY	2 Corinthians 6:14—7:1	*Believers are called out*
SATURDAY	Psalm 86	*Walking in God's way*

Third Sunday after the Epiphany

SUNDAY	Jonah 3:1-5, 10	*Repentance at Nineveh*
	Psalm 62:5-12	*In God is my safety and my honor*
	1 Corinthians 7:29-31	*Living in the end times*
	Mark 1:14-20	*The calling of the disciples at the sea*
MONDAY	Genesis 12:1-9	*God calls Abram to go to Canaan*
TUESDAY	Genesis 45:25—46:7	*God calls Jacob to go to Egypt*
WEDNESDAY	Mark 3:13-19	*Jesus appoints the Twelve*
THURSDAY	Proverbs 8:1-21	*Wisdom calls the people*
FRIDAY	1 Corinthians 7:17-24	*Live the life assigned*
SATURDAY	Psalm 46	*The God of Jacob is our stronghold*

Fourth Sunday after the Epiphany

SUNDAY	Deuteronomy 18:15-20	*The prophet speaks with God's authority*
	Psalm 111	*The beginning of wisdom*
	1 Corinthians 8:1-13	*Limits to liberty*
	Mark 1:21-28	*The healing of one with an unclean spirit*
MONDAY	Numbers 22:1-21	*King Balak asks Balaam to curse Israel*
TUESDAY	Numbers 22:22-38	*An angel speaks God's word to Balaam*
WEDNESDAY	Mark 5:1-20	*Jesus heals a man with a demon*
THURSDAY	Jeremiah 29:1-14	*Jeremiah speaks God's word*
FRIDAY	1 Corinthians 7:32-40	*Paul on marriage*
SATURDAY	Psalm 35:1-10	*God is our salvation*

Fifth Sunday after the Epiphany

SUNDAY	Isaiah 40:21-31	*The Creator cares for the powerless*
	Psalm 147:1-11, 20c	*The LORD heals the brokenhearted*
	1 Corinthians 9:16-23	*A servant of the gospel*
	Mark 1:29-39	*The healing of Peter's mother-in-law*
MONDAY	2 Kings 4:8-17, 32-37	*Elijah raises the Shunamite child*
TUESDAY	2 Kings 8:1-6	*The Shunamite widow's land restored*
WEDNESDAY	Mark 3:7-12	*Jesus heals many people*
THURSDAY	Job 6:1-13	*Job's lament at misfortune*
FRIDAY	1 Corinthians 9:1-16	*An apostle's life*
SATURDAY	Psalm 102:12-28	*Prayer for healing*

Sixth Sunday after the Epiphany

SUNDAY	2 Kings 5:1-14	*Naaman is healed of leprosy*
	Psalm 30	*You restored me to health*
	1 Corinthians 9:24-27	*Run the race*
	Mark 1:40-45	*The healing of one with leprosy*
MONDAY	Leviticus 13:1-17	*The law concerning leprosy*
TUESDAY	Leviticus 14:1-20	*The purification of lepers*
WEDNESDAY	John 4:46-54	*Jesus heals a boy*
THURSDAY	Job 30:16-31	*Job's lament at his condition*
FRIDAY	1 Corinthians 10:14—11:1	*Do all to God's glory*
SATURDAY	Psalm 6	*Prayer for healing*

Seventh Sunday after the Epiphany

SUNDAY	Isaiah 43:18-25	*Rivers in the desert*
	Psalm 41	*Heal me, O God*
	2 Corinthians 1:18-22	*Every promise of God is a "Yes"*
	Mark 2:1-12	*The healing of a paralyzed man*
MONDAY	Isaiah 30:18-26	*God promises to heal*
TUESDAY	Micah 4:1-7	*God promises to restore*
WEDNESDAY	John 5:19-29	*The authority of the Son*
THURSDAY	Acts 14:8-18	*Paul heals a lame man*
FRIDAY	2 Corinthians 1:1-11	*Thanks after affliction*
SATURDAY	Psalm 38	*Prayer for health and forgiveness*

Eighth Sunday after the Epiphany

SUNDAY	Hosea 2:14-20	*The covenant renewed*
	Psalm 103:1-13, 22	*God's compassion and mercy*
	2 Corinthians 3:1-6	*Ministers of God's new covenant*
	Mark 2:13-22	*Eating with tax collectors and prostitutes*
MONDAY	Ezekiel 16:1-14	*God's beloved bride*
TUESDAY	Ezekiel 16:53-63	*God's everlasting covenant*
WEDNESDAY	John 3:22-36	*Christ, the bridegroom*
THURSDAY	Isaiah 62:1-5	*God marries the people*
FRIDAY	2 Corinthians 1:23—2:11	*About forgiveness*
SATURDAY	Psalm 45:6-17	*A marriage song*

The Transfiguration of Our Lord

SUNDAY	2 Kings 2:1-12	*Elijah taken up to heaven*
	Psalm 50:1-6	*God shines forth in glory*
	2 Corinthians 4:3-6	*God's light seen in Christ*
	Mark 9:2-9	*Christ revealed as God's beloved Son*
MONDAY	Exodus 19:7-25	*Moses meets God on the mountain*
TUESDAY	Job 19:23-27	*Job will see God*

Lent

Ash Wednesday

	Joel 2:1-2, 12-17	*Return to God*
	or Isaiah 58:1-12	*The fast that God chooses*
	Psalm 51:1-17	*A plea for mercy*
	2 Corinthians 5:20b—6:10	*Now is the day of salvation*
	Matthew 6:1-6, 16-21	*The practice of faith*
THURSDAY	Daniel 9:1-14	*Daniel prays for the people's forgiveness*
FRIDAY	Daniel 9:15-25a	*An angel speaks to Daniel*
SATURDAY	Psalm 32	*God forgives our sin*

First Sunday in Lent

SUNDAY	Genesis 9:8-17	*The rainbow, sign of God's covenant*
	Psalm 25:1-10	*Your paths are love and faithfulness*
	1 Peter 3:18-22	*Saved through water*
	Mark 1:9-15	*The temptation of Jesus*
MONDAY	Job 4:1-21	*Eliphaz speaks of sin*
TUESDAY	Job 5:8-27	*We are to seek God*
WEDNESDAY	Matthew 4:1-11	*Matthew's account of Jesus' temptation*
THURSDAY	Proverbs 30:1-9	*Plea to be safe from temptation*
FRIDAY	1 Peter 3:8-18a	*About suffering*
SATURDAY	Psalm 77	*Prayer for God to remember us*

Second Sunday in Lent

SUNDAY	Genesis 17:1-7, 15-16	*God blesses Abraham and Sarah*
	Psalm 22:23-31	*All the earth shall turn to God*
	Romans 4:13-25	*The promise to those of Abraham's faith*
	Mark 8:31-38	*The passion prediction*
MONDAY	Genesis 21:1-7	*God gives Abraham and Sarah a son*
TUESDAY	Genesis 22:1-19	*God asks Abraham to sacrifice Isaac*
WEDNESDAY	Mark 10:32-34	*Jesus foretells his death*
THURSDAY	Jeremiah 30:12-22	*God will restore Israel*
FRIDAY	Hebrews 11:1-3, 8-19	*By faith Abraham obeyed*
SATURDAY	Psalm 105:1-11, 37-45	*God promised life to Abraham*

Third Sunday in Lent

SUNDAY	Exodus 20:1-17	*The commandments given at Sinai*
	Psalm 19	*The commandments give light to the eyes*
	1 Corinthians 1:18-25	*Christ crucified, the wisdom of God*
	John 2:13-22	*The cleansing of the temple*
MONDAY	1 Kings 6:1-14, 21-22	*Solomon builds the temple*
TUESDAY	2 Chronicles 29:1-11, 16-19	*Hezekiah cleanses the temple*
WEDNESDAY	Mark 11:15-19	*Jesus cleanses the temple*
THURSDAY	Ezra 6:1-16	*King Darius orders the temple rebuilt*
FRIDAY	1 Corinthians 3:10-23	*You are God's temple*
SATURDAY	Psalm 84	*How lovely is God's dwelling place*

Fourth Sunday in Lent

SUNDAY	Numbers 21:4-9	*The lifting up of the serpent*
	Psalm 107:1-3, 17-22	*The LORD delivers from distress*
	Ephesians 2:1-10	*Alive in Christ*
	John 3:14-21	*The lifting up of the Son of Man*
MONDAY	Exodus 15:22-27	*God gives the people water*
TUESDAY	Numbers 20:1-13	*God gives water from the rock*
WEDNESDAY	John 8:12-20	*Christ the light of the world*
THURSDAY	Isaiah 60:15-22	*God is our light*
FRIDAY	Hebrews 3:1-6	*The faithfulness of Moses*
SATURDAY	Psalm 107:1-16	*God gives food and light*

Fifth Sunday in Lent

SUNDAY	Jeremiah 31:31-34	*A new covenant written on the heart*
	Psalm 51:1-12	*Create in me a clean heart*
	or Psalm 119:9-16	*I treasure your promise in my heart*
	Hebrews 5:5-10	*Through suffering Christ saves*
	John 12:20-33	*The grain of wheat dying in the earth*
MONDAY	Isaiah 43:8-13	*God is our savior*
TUESDAY	Isaiah 44:1-8	*God gives life to the people*
WEDNESDAY	John 12:34-50	*God gives eternal life*
THURSDAY	Haggai 2:1-9; 20-23	*God promises future blessings*
FRIDAY	2 Corinthians 3:4-11	*God's glory in Christ*
SATURDAY	Psalm 119:9-16	*Treasuring God's word*

Sunday of the Passion

PALM SUNDAY	Mark 11:1-11	*Hosanna*
	or John 12:12-16	*Entrance into the final days*
	Psalm 118:1-2, 19-29	*Blessed is the one who comes*
	Isaiah 50:4-9a	*The servant of the Lord suffers*
	Psalm 31:9-16	*I commend my spirit*
	Philippians 2:5-11	*Humbled to the point of death*
	Mark 14:1-15:47	*The passion and death of Jesus*
MONDAY	Psalm 10	*Prayer for destruction of the wicked*
TUESDAY	Psalm 44	*Prayer for protection from the wicked*
WEDNESDAY	Psalm 137	*We sat down and wept*

The Three Days

Maundy Thursday

Exodus 12:1-4 [5-10] 11-14	*The passover of the LORD*
Psalm 116:1-2, 12-19	*The cup of salvation*
1 Corinthians 11:23-26	*Proclaim the Lord's death until he comes*
John 13:1-17, 31b-35	*The service of Christ: footwashing and meal*

Good Friday

Isaiah 52:13—53:12	*The suffering servant*
Psalm 22	*My God, why have you forsaken me?*
Hebrews 10:16-25	*The way to God is opened by Jesus' death*
or Hebrews 4:14-16; 5:7-9	*Jesus, the merciful high priest*
John 18:1—19:42	*The passion and death of Jesus*

Holy Saturday

| Lamentations 3:1-9, 19-24 | *In God I hope* |

The Resurrection of Our Lord | Vigil of Easter

<table>
<tr><td rowspan="2">READINGS AND
RESPONSES</td><td>Genesis 1:1—2:4a</td><td>Creation</td></tr>
<tr><td>Psalm 136:1-9, 23-36</td><td>God's mercy endures forever</td></tr>
<tr><td></td><td>Genesis 7:1-5, 11-18; 8:6-18; 9:8-13</td><td>The flood</td></tr>
<tr><td></td><td>Psalm 46</td><td>The God of Jacob is our stronghold</td></tr>
<tr><td></td><td>Genesis 22:1-18</td><td>The testing of Abraham</td></tr>
<tr><td></td><td>Psalm 16</td><td>You will show me the path of life</td></tr>
<tr><td></td><td>Exodus 14:10-31; 15:20-21</td><td>Israel's deliverance at the Red Sea</td></tr>
<tr><td></td><td>Exodus 15:1b-13, 17-18</td><td>The LORD has triumphed gloriously</td></tr>
<tr><td></td><td>Isaiah 55:1-11</td><td>Salvation freely offered to all</td></tr>
<tr><td></td><td>Isaiah 12:2-6</td><td>The wells of salvation</td></tr>
<tr><td></td><td>Proverbs 8:1-8, 19-21; 9:4b-6</td><td></td></tr>
<tr><td></td><td>or Baruch 3:9-15, 32—4:4</td><td>The wisdom of God</td></tr>
<tr><td></td><td>Psalm 19</td><td>The law is just and rejoices in the heart</td></tr>
<tr><td></td><td>Ezekiel 36:24-28</td><td>A new heart and a new spirit</td></tr>
<tr><td></td><td>Psalm 42 and Psalm 43</td><td>My soul thirsts for the living God</td></tr>
<tr><td></td><td>Ezekiel 37:1-14</td><td>The valley of the dry bones</td></tr>
<tr><td></td><td>Psalm 143</td><td>Revive me, O LORD</td></tr>
<tr><td></td><td>Zephaniah 3:14-20</td><td>The gathering of God's people</td></tr>
<tr><td></td><td>Psalm 98</td><td>Lift up your voice, rejoice and sing</td></tr>
<tr><td></td><td>Jonah 3:1-10</td><td>The call of Jonah</td></tr>
<tr><td></td><td>Jonah 2:1-3 [4-6] 7-9</td><td>Deliverance belongs to our God</td></tr>
<tr><td></td><td>Deuteronomy 31:19-30</td><td>The song of Moses</td></tr>
<tr><td></td><td>Deuteronomy 32:1-4, 7, 36a, 43a</td><td>Justice for the people</td></tr>
<tr><td></td><td>Daniel 3:1-29</td><td>The fiery furnace</td></tr>
<tr><td></td><td>Song of the Three Young Men
3:35-65</td><td>Sing praise to the LORD</td></tr>
<tr><td></td><td>Romans 6:3-11</td><td>Dying and rising with Christ</td></tr>
<tr><td></td><td>Psalm 114</td><td>Tremble, O earth</td></tr>
<tr><td></td><td>Mark 16:1-8</td><td>The resurrection is announced</td></tr>
</table>

Easter

The Resurrection of Our Lord | Easter Day

<table>
<tr><td>SUNDAY</td><td>Acts 10:34-43</td><td>God raised Jesus on the third day</td></tr>
<tr><td></td><td>or Isaiah 25:6-9</td><td>The feast of victory</td></tr>
<tr><td></td><td>Psalm 118:1-2, 14-24</td><td>On this day the LORD has acted</td></tr>
<tr><td></td><td>1 Corinthians 15:1-11</td><td>Witnesses to the risen Christ</td></tr>
<tr><td></td><td>or Acts 10:34-43</td><td>God raised Jesus on the third day</td></tr>
<tr><td></td><td>John 20:1-18</td><td>Seeing the risen Christ</td></tr>
<tr><td></td><td>or Mark 16:1-8</td><td>The resurrection of Jesus is announced</td></tr>
</table>

The Resurrection of Our Lord | Easter Evening

SUNDAY	Isaiah 25:6-9	*The feast of victory*
	Psalm 114	*Hallelujah*
	1 Corinthians 5:6b-8	*Celebrating with sincerity and truth*
	Luke 24:13-49	*At evening, the risen Christ is revealed*
MONDAY	Genesis 1:1—2:4a	*The creation of the world*
TUESDAY	Psalm 104:1-24	*The works of God*
WEDNESDAY	Mark 16:1-8	*Mark's account of the resurrection*
THURSDAY	Song of Solomon 3:1-11	*The song of the lover*
FRIDAY	1 Corinthians 15:35-58	*The resurrected body*
SATURDAY	Psalm 136	*God's steadfast love*

Second Sunday of Easter

SUNDAY	Acts 4:32-35	*The believers' common life*
	Psalm 133	*How good it is to live in unity*
	1 John 1:1—2:2	*Walking in the light*
	John 20:19-31	*Beholding the wounds of the risen Christ*
MONDAY	Daniel 3:1-30	*God saves the three men from the fire*
TUESDAY	Daniel 6:1-28	*God saves Daniel from the lions*
WEDNESDAY	Mark 12:18-27	*Jesus teaches about the resurrection*
THURSDAY	Isaiah 26:1-15	*Song of victory*
FRIDAY	1 John 2:3-17	*A new commandment*
SATURDAY	Psalm 135	*Praise to God*

Third Sunday of Easter

SUNDAY	Acts 3:12-19	*Health and forgiveness through Jesus*
	Psalm 4	*The LORD does wonders for the faithful*
	1 John 3:1-7	*The revealing of the children of God*
	Luke 24:36b-48	*Eating with the risen Christ*
MONDAY	Jeremiah 30:1-11a	*God will save the people*
TUESDAY	Daniel 10:2-19	*Daniel's vision strengthens him*
WEDNESDAY	Mark 16:9-18	*Jesus appears to the disciples*
THURSDAY	Hosea 5:15—6:6	*Salvation on the third day*
FRIDAY	1 John 3:7-15	*Love one another*
SATURDAY	Psalm 150	*Praise to God*

Fourth Sunday of Easter

SUNDAY	Acts 4:5-12	*Salvation in the name of Jesus*
	Psalm 23	*The LORD is my shepherd*
	1 John 3:16-24	*Love in truth and action*
	John 10:11-18	*Christ, the shepherd*
MONDAY	Genesis 48:8-19	*God has been my shepherd*
TUESDAY	1 Chronicles 11:1-9	*The shepherd David made king*
WEDNESDAY	Mark 14:26-31	*Christ, the shepherd*
THURSDAY	Micah 7:8-20	*God will shepherd the people*
FRIDAY	1 Peter 5:1-5	*Christ, the great shepherd*
SATURDAY	Psalm 95	*We are the sheep of God's hand*

Fifth Sunday of Easter

SUNDAY	Acts 8:26-40	*Philip teaches and baptizes an Ethiopian*
	Psalm 22:25-31	*All shall turn to the LORD*
	1 John 4:7-21	*Loving one another*
	John 15:1-8	*Christ, the vine*
MONDAY	Isaiah 5:1-7	*The unfaithful vineyard*
TUESDAY	Isaiah 32:9-20	*A fruitful field*
WEDNESDAY	John 14:18-31	*Keeping God's word*
THURSDAY	Isaiah 65:17-25	*God's people like a tree*
FRIDAY	Galatians 5:16-26	*The fruits of the Spirit*
SATURDAY	Psalm 80	*Israel, the vine*

Sixth Sunday of Easter

SUNDAY	Acts 10:44-48	*The Spirit poured out on the Gentiles*
	Psalm 98	*Shout with joy to the LORD*
	1 John 5:1-6	*The victory of faith*
	John 15:9-17	*Christ, the friend and lover*
MONDAY	Deuteronomy 7:1-11	*Keeping God's commandments*
TUESDAY	Deuteronomy 11:1-17	*The rewards of obedience*
WEDNESDAY	Mark 16:19-20	*Mark's account of the ascension*

The Ascension of Our Lord

	Acts 1:1-11	*Jesus sends the apostles*
	Psalm 47	*God has gone up with a shout*
	or Psalm 93	*God's throne has been established*
	Ephesians 1:15-23	*Seeing the risen and ascended Christ*
	Luke 24:44-53	*Christ present in all times and places*
FRIDAY	Revelation 1:9-18	*A vision of the risen Christ*
SATURDAY	Psalm 132	*The crowning of the son of David*

Seventh Sunday of Easter

SUNDAY	Acts 1:15-17, 21-26	*Matthias added to the apostles*
	Psalm 1	*The way of the righteous*
	1 John 5:9-13	*Life in the Son of God*
	John 17:6-19	*Christ's prayer for his disciples*
MONDAY	Exodus 28:29-38	*The priest Aaron prays for the people*
TUESDAY	Numbers 8:5-22	*The Levites consecrated for service*
WEDNESDAY	John 16:16-24	*Sorrow turned to joy*
THURSDAY	Ezra 9:5-15	*Ezra prays for the people*
FRIDAY	3 John 1-15	*Love within the community*
SATURDAY	Psalm 115	*God's blessings on the chosen ones*

Vigil of Pentecost

Exodus 19:1-9	*The covenant at Sinai*
or Acts 2:1-11	*Filled with the Spirit*
Psalm 33:12-22	*The Lord is our help and our shield*
or Psalm 130	*There is forgiveness*
Romans 8:14-17, 22-27	*Praying with the Spirit*
John 7:37-39	*Jesus, the true living water*

The Day of Pentecost

SUNDAY	Acts 2:1-21	*Filled with the Spirit*
	or Ezekiel 37:1-14	*Life to dry bones*
	Psalm 104:24-34, 35b	*Renewing the face of the earth*
	Romans 8:22-27	*Praying with the Spirit*
	or Acts 2:1-21	*Filled with the Spirit*
	John 15:26-27; 16:4b-15	*Christ sends the Spirit of truth*
MONDAY	Joel 2:18-29	*God's spirit poured out*
TUESDAY	Ezekiel 37:1-14	*Dry bones alive with God's spirit*
WEDNESDAY	John 7:37-39	*The living water of the Spirit*
THURSDAY	Genesis 11:1-9	*The fragmenting of human tongues*
FRIDAY	1 Corinthians 12:4-27	*Many gifts, one Spirit*
SATURDAY	Psalm 149	*The faithful exult in God's glory*

41

Sundays after Pentecost

The Holy Trinity

SUNDAY	Isaiah 6:1-8	*Isaiah's vision and call*
	Psalm 29	*Worship God in holiness*
	Romans 8:12-17	*Living by the Spirit*
	John 3:1-17	*Entering the reign of God*
MONDAY	Numbers 9:15-23	*God in the cloud and the fire*
TUESDAY	Exodus 25:1-22	*God in the ark and its mercy seat*
WEDNESDAY	Mark 4:21-25	*Secrets will come to light*
THURSDAY	Numbers 6:22-27	*Aaronic blessing*
FRIDAY	Revelation 4:1-11	*Heaven's song of holy, holy, holy*
SATURDAY	Psalm 20	*The name of God*

Sunday between May 24 and 28 inclusive (Proper 3)

SUNDAY	Hosea 2:14-20	*The covenant renewed*
	Psalm 103:1-13, 22	*The LORD is merciful*
	2 Corinthians 3:1-6	*Ministers of God's new covenant*
	Mark 2:13-22	*Eating with tax collectors and prostitutes*

Sunday between May 29 and June 4 inclusive (Proper 4)

SUNDAY	Deuteronomy 5:12-15	*The commandment regarding the sabbath*
	Psalm 81:1-10	*Raise a loud shout to the God of Jacob*
	or 1 Samuel 3:1-10 [11-20]	*The calling of Samuel*
	Psalm 139:1-6, 13-18	*You have searched me out*
	or Psalm 46	*The God of Jacob is our stronghold*
	2 Corinthians 4:5-12	*Treasure in clay jars*
	Mark 2:23—3:6	*Doing the work of God on the sabbath*
MONDAY	Exodus 31:12-18	*The sabbath law*
TUESDAY	Exodus 16:13-26	*Concerning food on the sabbath*
WEDNESDAY	John 5:1-18	*Jesus heals on the sabbath*
THURSDAY	1 Samuel 21:1-6	*David eats the bread of the Presence*
FRIDAY	Acts 15:1-5, 22-35	*The church considers Jewish practices*
SATURDAY	Psalm 78:1-4, 52-72	*God's care for the chosen people*

Sunday between June 5 and 11 inclusive (Proper 5)

SUNDAY	Genesis 3:8-15	*God confronts Adam and Eve*
	Psalm 130	*With you there is forgiveness*
	or 1 Samuel 8:4-11[12-15]16-20	
	[11:14-15]	*Israel desires a king*
	Psalm 138	*Your love endures forever*
	2 Corinthians 4:13—5:1	*Renewed in the inner nature*
	Mark 3:20-35	*Doing the work of God*
MONDAY	1 Samuel 16:14-23	*David calms Saul's evil spirit*
TUESDAY	1 Kings 18:17-40	*Elijah destroys the evil prophets*
WEDNESDAY	Luke 11:14-28	*Jesus and Beelzebul*
THURSDAY	Isaiah 26:16—27:1	*God destroys Leviathan*
FRIDAY	Revelation 20:1-15	*Satan's doom*
SATURDAY	Psalm 74	*God will save us from the enemy*

Sunday between June 12 and 18 inclusive (Proper 6)

SUNDAY	Ezekiel 17:22-24	*The sign of the cedar*
	Psalm 92:1-4, 12-15	*The righteous are like a cedar of Lebanon*
	or 1 Samuel 15:34—16:13	*David anointed by Samuel*
	Psalm 20	*Victory to the anointed one*
	2 Corinthians 5:6-10 [11-13] 14-17	*In Christ, a new creation*
	Mark 4:26-34	*The parable of the mustard seed*
MONDAY	Ezekiel 31:1-12	*Evil can be a towering cedar*
TUESDAY	Jeremiah 22:1-9	*The evil will be cut down*
WEDNESDAY	Mark 4:1-20	*The parable of the sower*
THURSDAY	Genesis 3:14-24	*Deprived of the tree of life*
FRIDAY	Revelation 21:22—22:5	*Given the tree of life*
SATURDAY	Psalm 52	*Like an olive tree in God's house*

Sunday between June 19 and 25 inclusive (Proper 7)

SUNDAY	Job 38:1-11	*The Creator of earth and sea*
	Psalm 107:1-3, 23-32	*God stilled the storm*
	or 1 Samuel 17:[1a, 4-11, 19-23]	
	32-49	*David's victory over Goliath*
	Psalm 9:9-20	*You are a refuge in time of trouble*
	or 1 Samuel 17:57-18:5, 10-16	*David and Jonathan*
	Psalm 133	*How good it is to live in unity*
	2 Corinthians 6:1-13	*Paul's defense of his ministry*
	Mark 4:35-41	*Christ calming the sea*
MONDAY	Exodus 7:14-24	*God turns the Nile into blood*
TUESDAY	Exodus 9:13-35	*God sends hail*
WEDNESDAY	Mark 6:45-52	*Jesus walks on the water*
THURSDAY	Joshua 10:1-14	*God makes the sun stand still*
FRIDAY	Acts 27:13-38	*Paul and the storm at sea*
SATURDAY	Psalm 65	*God silences the seas*

Sunday between June 26 and July 2 inclusive (Proper 8)

SUNDAY	Lamentations 3:23-33	*Great is the LORD's faithfulness*
	or Wisdom 1:13-15; 2:23-24	*God created humankind for immortality*
	Psalm 30	*You have lifted me up*
	or 2 Samuel 1:1, 17-27	*Lamentation over Saul and Jonathan*
	Psalm 130	*Out of the depths I cry to you*
	2 Corinthians 8:7-15	*Excel in generosity, following the Lord Jesus*
	Mark 5:21-43	*Christ heals a woman and Jairus' daughter*
MONDAY	Leviticus 21:1-15	*Dead bodies are unclean*
TUESDAY	Leviticus 15:19-31	*Bleeding women are unclean*
WEDNESDAY	Mark 9:14-29	*Jesus heals a child*
THURSDAY	2 Kings 20:1-11	*God heals Hezekiah*
FRIDAY	2 Corinthians 7:2-16	*Grief leads to repentance*
SATURDAY	Psalm 88	*Prayer for restoration*

Sunday between July 3 and 9 inclusive (Proper 9)

SUNDAY	Ezekiel 2:1-5	*The call of Ezekiel*
	Psalm 123	*Our eyes look to you, O God*
	or 2 Samuel 5:1-5, 9-10	*The reign of David*
	Psalm 48	*God shall be our guide forevermore*
	2 Corinthians 12:2-10	*God's power made perfect in weakness*
	Mark 6:1-13	*Sending the Twelve to preach and heal*
MONDAY	Jeremiah 16:1-13	*Jeremiah's celibacy and message*
TUESDAY	Jeremiah 16:14-21	*God will forgive Israel*
WEDNESDAY	John 7:1-9	*Unbelief of Jesus' brothers*
THURSDAY	Ezekiel 2:8—3:11	*Ezekiel to eat the scroll*
FRIDAY	2 Corinthians 11:16-33	*Paul's sufferings*
SATURDAY	Psalm 119:81-88	*The faithful persecuted*

Sunday between July 10 and 16 inclusive (Proper 10)

SUNDAY	Amos 7:7-15	*The sign of the plumb line*
	Psalm 85:8-13	*Listen to what the LORD God is saying*
	or 2 Samuel 6:1-5, 12b-19	*David dances before the ark*
	Psalm 24	*Lift up your head*
	Ephesians 1:3-14	*Chosen to live in praise of God*
	Mark 6:14-29	*The death of John the Baptist*
MONDAY	Amos 2:6-16	*Amos condemns Israel*
TUESDAY	Amos 4:6-13	*Prepare to meet your God*
WEDNESDAY	Luke 1:57-80	*The birth of John the Baptist*
THURSDAY	Acts 21:27-39	*Paul arrested*
FRIDAY	Acts 23:12-35	*Plot to kill Paul*
SATURDAY	Psalm 142	*Prayer for deliverance*

Sunday between July 17 and 23 inclusive (Proper 11)

SUNDAY	Jeremiah 23:1-6	*A righteous shepherd for Israel*
	Psalm 23	*The LORD is my shepherd*
	or 2 Samuel 7:1-14a	*God's promise to David*
	Psalm 89:20-37	*I will sing of your love*
	Ephesians 2:11-22	*Reconciled to God through Christ*
	Mark 6:30-34, 53-56	*Christ healing the multitudes*
MONDAY	Jeremiah 50:1-7	*God the true pasture*
TUESDAY	Zechariah 9:14—10:2	*God will save the flock*
WEDNESDAY	Luke 15:1-7	*Parable of the lost sheep*
THURSDAY	2 Samuel 5:1-12	*David is to shepherd Israel*
FRIDAY	Acts 20:16-38	*The elders are shepherds*
SATURDAY	Psalm 100	*We are God's sheep*

Sunday between July 24 and 30 inclusive (Proper 12)

SUNDAY	2 Kings 4:42-44	*Elisha feeds a hundred people*
	Psalm 145:10-18	*You open wide your hand*
	or 2 Samuel 11:1-15	*Bathsheba and Uriah wronged by David*
	Psalm 14	*God in the company of the righteous*
	Ephesians 3:14-21	*Prayer to Christ*
	John 6:1-21	*Jesus feeds the 5000*
MONDAY	Genesis 18:1-14	*God eats with Abraham and Sarah*
TUESDAY	Exodus 24:1-11	*The elders eat with God*
WEDNESDAY	Mark 6:35-44	*Jesus feeds 5000*
THURSDAY	Isaiah 25:6-10	*A feast on the mountain*
FRIDAY	Philippians 4:10-20	*Christian generosity*
SATURDAY	Psalm 111	*God gives food*

Sunday between July 31 and August 6 inclusive (Proper 13)

SUNDAY	Exodus 16:2-4, 9-15	*Manna in the wilderness*
	Psalm 78:23-29	*Manna rains down*
	or 2 Samuel 11:26—12:13a	*David rebuked by Nathan*
	Psalm 51:1-12	*Have mercy on me, O God*
	Ephesians 4:1-16	*Maintain the unity of the faith*
	John 6:24-35	*Christ, the bread of life*
MONDAY	Numbers 11:16-23, 31-32	*God sends quail*
TUESDAY	Deuteronomy 8:1-20	*You will eat your fill*
WEDNESDAY	Mark 8:1-10	*Jesus feeds 4000*
THURSDAY	Isaiah 55:1-9	*Come and eat*
FRIDAY	Ephesians 4:17-24	*The new life*
SATURDAY	Psalm 107:1-3, 33-43	*God feeds the hungry*

Sunday between August 7 and 13 inclusive (Proper 14)

SUNDAY	1 Kings 19:4-8	*Elijah receives bread for his journey*
	Psalm 34:1-8	*Taste and see that the LORD is good*
	or 2 Samuel 18:5-9, 15, 31-33	*David laments Absalom's death*
	Psalm 130	*Out of the depths I cry to you*
	Ephesians 4:25—5:2	*Put away evil, live in love*
	John 6:35, 41-51	*Christ, the bread of life*
MONDAY	1 Kings 17:1-16	*God feeds the widow of Zarephath*
TUESDAY	Ruth 2:1-23	*Ruth gleans in Boaz's fields*
WEDNESDAY	John 6:35-40	*Doing God's will*
THURSDAY	Jeremiah 31:1-6	*God promises fruitful vineyards*
FRIDAY	Ephesians 5:1-14	*Fruits of the light*
SATURDAY	Psalm 81	*God will feed us*

Sunday between August 14 and 20 inclusive (Proper 15)

SUNDAY	Proverbs 9:1-6	*Invited to dine at wisdom's feast*
	Psalm 34:9-14	*Seeking God*
	or 1 Kings 2:10-12; 3:3-14	*Solomon's prayer for wisdom*
	Psalm 111	*The beginning of wisdom*
	Ephesians 5:15-20	*Filled with the Spirit*
	John 6:51-58	*Christ, the true food and drink*
MONDAY	Genesis 43:1-15	*Joseph's brothers need food*
TUESDAY	Genesis 45:1-15	*Joseph provides food*
WEDNESDAY	Mark 8:14-21	*Jesus teaches about bread*
THURSDAY	Genesis 47:13-26	*Famine even in Egypt*
FRIDAY	Acts 6:1-7	*Deacons chosen to distribute food*
SATURDAY	Psalm 36	*God saves humans and animals alike*

Sunday between August 21 and 27 inclusive (Proper 16)

SUNDAY	Joshua 24:1-2a, 14-18	*Serve the LORD*
	Psalm 34:15-22	*The eyes of God are upon the righteous*
	or 1 Kings 8:[1, 6, 10-11]	
	22-30, 41-43	*Solomon's prayer at the temple dedication*
	Psalm 84	*Your dwelling is dear to me*
	Ephesians 6:10-20	*Put on the armor of God*
	John 6:56-69	*The bread of eternal life*
MONDAY	Nehemiah 9:1-15	*Nehemiah praises God's care of the people*
TUESDAY	Nehemiah 9:16-31	*Nehemiah confesses the people's sin*
WEDNESDAY	John 15:16-25	*Keeping God's word*
THURSDAY	Isaiah 33:10-16	*The righteous will eat*
FRIDAY	Ephesians 5:21—6:9	*A household code*
SATURDAY	Psalm 119:97-104	*God's word is sweet*

Sunday between Aug. 28 and Sept. 3 inclusive (Proper 17)

SUNDAY	Deuteronomy 4:1-2, 6-9	*God's law: a sign of a great nation*
	Psalm 15	*Dwelling in God's tabernacle*
	or Song of Solomon 2:8-13	*Song of two lovers*
	Psalm 45:1-2, 6-9	*The oil of gladness*
	James 1:17-27	*Be doers of the word*
	Mark 7:1-8, 14-15, 21-23	*Authentic religion*
MONDAY	Exodus 32:1-14	*The Israelites make themselves a god*
TUESDAY	Exodus 32:15-35	*Moses punishes their evil*
WEDNESDAY	Mark 7:9-23	*Jesus teaches about tradition*
THURSDAY	Deuteronomy 4:21-40	*Moses urges faithfulness*
FRIDAY	James 1:1-16	*Trials and temptations*
SATURDAY	Psalm 106:1-6, 13-23, 47-48	*God will remember the people*

Sunday between September 4 and 10 inclusive (Proper 18)

SUNDAY	Isaiah 35:4-7a	*God comes with healing*
	Psalm 146	*Praising the LORD*
	or Proverbs 22:1-2, 8-9, 22-23	*Sayings concerning a good name*
	Psalm 125	*Trusting in God*
	James 2:1-10 [11-13] 14-17	*Faith without works is dead*
	Mark 7:24-37	*Christ heals a little girl and a deaf man*
MONDAY	Joshua 6:1-21	*The Israelites conquer Jericho*
TUESDAY	Joshua 8:1-22	*The Israelites conquer Ai*
WEDNESDAY	Matthew 17:14-21	*Healing by faith*
THURSDAY	Judges 15:9-20	*Samson slays the Philistines*
FRIDAY	Hebrews 11:29—12:2	*The heroes of faith*
SATURDAY	Isaiah 38:10-20	*Prayer for health*

Sunday between September 11 and 17 inclusive (Proper 19)

SUNDAY	Isaiah 50:4-9a	*The servant is vindicated by God*
	Psalm 116:1-9	*I will walk in God's presence*
	or Proverbs 1:20-33	*Wisdom's rebuke to the foolish*
	Psalm 19	*The law is just and rejoices the heart*
	or Wisdom 7:26—8:1	*The one who lives with wisdom*
	James 3:1-12	*Dangers of the unbridled tongue*
	Mark 8:27-38	*Peter's confession of faith*
MONDAY	1 Kings 13:1-10	*Obeying the word of God*
TUESDAY	1 Kings 13:11-25	*Disobeying the word of God*
WEDNESDAY	John 7:25-36	*Jesus the messiah*
THURSDAY	Isaiah 10:12-20	*Evil will be destroyed*
FRIDAY	James 2:17-26	*The works of faith*
SATURDAY	Psalm 119:169-176	*God's law my delight*

Sunday between September 18 and 24 inclusive (Proper 20)

SUNDAY	Jeremiah 11:18-20	*The prophet is like a lamb*
	or Wisdom 1:16—2:1, 12-22	*The righteous shall live*
	Psalm 54	*God is my helper*
	or Proverbs 31:10-31	*The capable wife*
	Psalm 1	*Delight in God's law*
	James 3:13—4:3, 7-8a	*The wisdom from above*
	Mark 9:30-37	*Prediction of the passion*
MONDAY	2 Kings 5:1-13	*The girl servant saves her master*
TUESDAY	2 Kings 11:21—12:16	*The boy king repairs the temple*
WEDNESDAY	John 8:21-38	*Being disciples of Jesus*
THURSDAY	Jeremiah 1:4-10	*God calls Jeremiah while in the womb*
FRIDAY	James 4:8—5:6	*Draw near to God*
SATURDAY	Psalm 139:1-18	*God formed me in my mother's womb*

Sunday between Sept. 25 and Oct. 1 inclusive (Proper 21)

SUNDAY	Numbers 11:4-6, 10-16, 24-29	*The spirit upon seventy elders*
	Psalm 19:7-14	*The law gives light*
	or Esther 7:1-6, 9-10; 9:20-22	*Esther's intercession*
	Psalm 124	*We have escaped like a bird*
	James 5:13-20	*Prayer and anointing in the community*
	Mark 9:38-50	*Warnings to those who obstruct faith*
MONDAY	Exodus 18:13-27	*Moses appoints judges to keep peace*
TUESDAY	Deuteronomy 1:1-18	*Moses charges the judges*
WEDNESDAY	Matthew 5:13-20	*You are salt and light*
THURSDAY	Zechariah 10:1-12	*God will gather the people*
FRIDAY	Acts 4:13-31	*The believers pray for boldness*
SATURDAY	Psalm 5	*Lead me in righteousness*

Sunday between October 2 and 8 inclusive (Proper 22)

SUNDAY	Genesis 2:18-24	*Created for relationship*
	Psalm 8	*You adorn us with glory and honor*
	or Job 1:1; 2:1-10	*Job's integrity in suffering*
	Psalm 26	*Your love is before my eyes*
	Hebrews 1:1-4; 2:5-12	*God has spoken by a Son*
	Mark 10:2-16	*Teaching on marriage*
MONDAY	Deuteronomy 22:13-30	*Laws about sexual relations*
TUESDAY	Deuteronomy 24:1-5	*Laws about divorce*
WEDNESDAY	Matthew 5:27-48	*Be perfect*
THURSDAY	Jeremiah 3:6-14	*God will forgive the unfaithful people*
FRIDAY	1 Corinthians 7:1-16	*Paul on marriage and divorce*
SATURDAY	Psalm 112	*Happy those who fear God*

Sunday between October 9 and 15 inclusive (Proper 23)

SUNDAY	Amos 5:6-7, 10-15	*Turn from injustice to the poor*
	Psalm 90:12-17	*Teach us to number our days*
	or Job 23:1-9, 16-17	*The Almighty hidden from Job*
	Psalm 22:1-15	*My God, why have you forsaken me?*
	Hebrews 4:12-16	*Approach the throne of grace*
	Mark 10:17-31	*Teaching on wealth and reward*
MONDAY	Deuteronomy 5:1-21	*The Ten Commandments*
TUESDAY	Deuteronomy 5:22-33	*Moses mediates God's word to the people*
WEDNESDAY	Matthew 15:1-9	*Jesus teaches the true commandments*
THURSDAY	Amos 3:13—4:5	*Judgment against oppressors*
FRIDAY	Hebrews 3:7—4:11	*Against disobedience*
SATURDAY	Psalm 26	*Prayer for acceptance*

Sunday between October 16 and 22 inclusive (Proper 24)

SUNDAY	Isaiah 53:4-12	*The suffering servant*
	Psalm 91:9-16	*The Most High, your refuge and habitation*
	or Job 38:1-7 [34-41]	*Challenges to Job from God*
	Psalm 104:1-9, 24, 35c	*How manifold are your works*
	Hebrews 5:1-10	*Through suffering Christ saves*
	Mark 10:35-45	*Warnings to ambitious disciples*
MONDAY	1 Samuel 8:1-18	*Samuel warns against kings*
TUESDAY	1 Samuel 10:17-25	*Saul proclaimed king anyway*
WEDNESDAY	John 13:1-17	*Jesus washes the disciples' feet*
THURSDAY	Genesis 14:17-24	*The story of Melchizedek*
FRIDAY	Hebrews 6:1-20	*The hope of God's promise*
SATURDAY	Psalm 37:23-40	*God will exalt the righteous*

Sunday between October 23 and 29 inclusive (Proper 25)

SUNDAY	Jeremiah 31:7-9	*The remnant of Israel gathered*
	Psalm 126	*Sowing with tears, reaping with joy*
	or Job 42:1-6, 10-17	*Job's restoration*
	Psalm 34:1-8 [19-22]	*Taste the LORD's goodness*
	Hebrews 7:23-28	*Christ, the merciful high priest*
	Mark 10:46-52	*Christ heals blind Bartimaeus*
MONDAY	Exodus 4:1-17	*Moses' power from God*
TUESDAY	2 Kings 6:8-24	*Elisha has power over sight*
WEDNESDAY	Mark 8:22-26	*Jesus heals a blind man*
THURSDAY	Jeremiah 33:1-11	*God promises healing*
FRIDAY	Hebrews 7:1-22	*Jesus like Melchizedek*
SATURDAY	Psalm 119:17-24	*Open my eyes*

Sunday between Oct. 30 and Nov. 5 inclusive (Proper 26)

SUNDAY	Deuteronomy 6:1-9	*Keeping the words of God*
	Psalm 119:1-8	*Seeking God with all our hearts*
	or Ruth 1:1-18	*Ruth remains with Naomi*
	Psalm 146	*The LORD lifts those bowed down*
	Hebrews 9:11-14	*Redeemed through Christ's blood*
	Mark 12:28-34	*Two commandments: love God and neighbor*
MONDAY	Deuteronomy 6:10-25	*Keeping the commandments*
TUESDAY	Deuteronomy 28:58—29:1	*Warnings against disobedience*
WEDNESDAY	John 13:31-35	*Commandment to love one another*
THURSDAY	Micah 6:1-8	*Command to do justice*
FRIDAY	Hebrews 9:1-12	*Temple sacrifices and Christ*
SATURDAY	Psalm 51	*A contrite heart*

Sunday between November 6 and 12 inclusive (Proper 27)

SUNDAY	1 Kings 17:8-16	*God feeds Elijah and the widow*
	Psalm 146	*The LORD lifts those bowed down*
	or Ruth 3:1-5; 4:13-17	*Ruth wins the favor of Boaz*
	Psalm 127	*Children are given by God*
	Hebrews 9:24-28	*The sacrifice of Christ*
	Mark 12:38-44	*A widow's generosity*
MONDAY	Ruth 1:1-22	*The widow's poverty*
TUESDAY	Ruth 4:7-22	*The widow's life restored*
WEDNESDAY	Mark 11:12-14, 20-24	*Condemnation and blessing*
THURSDAY	Deuteronomy 24:17-22	*Laws concerning the poor*
FRIDAY	Hebrews 9:15-24	*The blood of the old covenant*
SATURDAY	Psalm 94	*God will vindicate the righteous*

Sunday between November 13 and 19 inclusive (Proper 28)

SUNDAY	Daniel 12:1-3	*God will deliver the people*
	Psalm 16	*My heart is glad*
	or 1 Samuel 1:4-20	*Hannah's prayers answered*
	1 Samuel 2:1-10	*My heart exults in God*
	Hebrews 10:11-14 [15-18] 19-25	*The way to God through Christ*
	Mark 13:1-8	*The end and the coming of the Son*
MONDAY	Daniel 4:4-18	*Nebuchadnezzar's dream*
TUESDAY	Daniel 4:19-27, 34-37	*Nebuchadnezzer cut down*
WEDNESDAY	Mark 13:9-23	*The coming sufferings*
THURSDAY	Zechariah 12:1—13:1	*The future of Jerusalem*
FRIDAY	Hebrews 10:26-39	*Call for endurance*
SATURDAY	Psalm 13	*Prayer for salvation*

Christ the King (Proper 29)

SUNDAY	Daniel 7:9-10, 13-14	*The coming one rules over all*
	Psalm 93	*Your throne has been established*
	or 2 Samuel 23:1-7	*The just ruler like morning light*
	Psalm 132:1-12 [13-18]	*The faithful people sing with joy*
	Revelation 1:4b-8	*Christ, the ruler of the earth*
	John 18:33-37	*The kingdom of Christ*
MONDAY	Daniel 7:1-8, 15-18	*Daniel's vision of four beasts*
TUESDAY	Daniel 7:19-27	*The holy ones receive the kingdom*
WEDNESDAY	John 16:25-33	*Jesus speaking in figures*
THURSDAY	Ezekiel 28:20-26	*Israel will be safe*
FRIDAY	Revelation 11:7-19	*God's reign at the end of time*
SATURDAY	Psalm 76	*God is victorious*

Cycle C

Cycle C

First Sunday in Advent

SUNDAY	Jeremiah 33:14-16	*A righteous branch springs from David*
	Psalm 25:1-10	*To you, I lift up my soul*
	1 Thessalonians 3:9-13	*Strengthen hearts of holiness*
	Luke 21:25-36	*Watch for the coming of the Son of Man*
MONDAY	Numbers 17:1-11	*The budding of Aaron's rod*
TUESDAY	2 Samuel 7:18-29	*The flowering of David's line*
WEDNESDAY	Luke 11:29-32	*The coming of the Son of Man*
THURSDAY	Isaiah 1:24-31	*Warning not to wither*
FRIDAY	2 Peter 3:1-18	*Growing in grace*
SATURDAY	Psalm 90	*Prayer for life from God*

Second Sunday in Advent

SUNDAY	Malachi 3:1-4	*The messenger refines and purifies*
	or Baruch 5:1-9	*The return of scattered Israel*
	Luke 1:68-79	*God's tender compassion*
	Philippians 1:3-11	*A harvest of righteousness*
	Luke 3:1-6	*Prepare the way of the Lord*
MONDAY	Isaiah 40:1-11	*The earth prepares for God*
TUESDAY	Isaiah 19:18-25	*All nations shall praise God*
WEDNESDAY	Luke 7:18-30	*John the Baptist questions Jesus*
THURSDAY	Numbers 3:5-13	*The duties of the Levites*
FRIDAY	2 Peter 1:2-15	*Living God's call*
SATURDAY	Psalm 126	*Prayer for restoration*

Third Sunday in Advent

SUNDAY	Zephaniah 3:14-20	*Rejoice in God*
	Isaiah 12:2-6	*In your midst is the Holy One of Israel*
	Philippians 4:4-7	*Rejoice, the Lord is near*
	Luke 3:7-18	*One more powerful is coming*
MONDAY	Numbers 16:1-19	*Korah's company rebels*
TUESDAY	Numbers 16:20-35	*God destroys Korah's company*
WEDNESDAY	Luke 7:31-35	*The Messiah and John the Baptist*
THURSDAY	Micah 4:8-13	*God will thresh out the people*
FRIDAY	Acts 28:23-31	*Paul preaches in Rome*
SATURDAY	Psalm 85	*Prayer for mercy*

Fourth Sunday in Advent

SUNDAY	Micah 5:2-5a	*From Bethlehem comes a ruler*
	Luke 1:47-55	*God lifts up the lowly*
	or Psalm 80:1-7	*Show the light of your countenance*
	Hebrews 10:5-10	*I have come to do your will*
	Luke 1:39-45 [46-55]	*Blessed are you among women*
MONDAY	Genesis 25:19-28	*Rebekah bears Jacob and Esau*
TUESDAY	Genesis 30:1-24	*Leah and Rachel bear their sons*
WEDNESDAY	Luke 1:5-25	*Elizabeth will bear a child*
THURSDAY	Isaiah 42:14-21	*God is like a woman in labor*
FRIDAY	Romans 8:18-30	*The whole creation is in labor*
SATURDAY	Psalm 113	*Praise to God*

Christmas

The Nativity of Our Lord | Christmas Eve

DECEMBER 24	Isaiah 9:2-7	*A child is born for us*
	Psalm 96	*Let the earth be glad*
	Titus 2:11-14	*The grace of God has appeared*
	Luke 2:1-14 [15-20]	*God with us*

The Nativity of Our Lord | Christmas Dawn

DECEMBER 25	Isaiah 62:6-12	*God comes to restore the people*
	Psalm 97	*Light springs up for the righteous*
	Titus 3:4-7	*Saved through water and the Spirit*
	Luke 2:[1-7] 8-20	*The birth of the Messiah revealed to shepherds*

The Nativity of Our Lord | Christmas Day

DECEMBER 25	Isaiah 52:7-20	*Heralds announce God's salvation*
	Psalm 98	*The victory of our God*
	Hebrews 1:1-4 [5-12]	*God has spoken by a son*
	John 1:1-14	*The Word became flesh*
DECEMBER 26	Luke 2:1-20	*Luke's story of Jesus' birth*
DECEMBER 27	Luke 3:23-38	*Luke's genealogy*
DECEMBER 28	Psalm 148	*All creation praises God*
DECEMBER 29	Genesis 1:1—2:4a	*The creation of the world*
DECEMBER 30	Psalm 150	*Praise to God*
DECEMBER 31	Hebrews 1:1—2:4	*The Son of God appears*

The Name of Jesus

JANUARY 1	Numbers 6:22-27	*The Aaronic blessing*
	Psalm 8	*How exalted is your name*
	Galatians 4:4-7	*We are no longer slaves*
	or Philippians 2:5-11	*God takes on human form*
	Luke 2:15-21	*The child is named Jesus*

First Sunday after Christmas

SUNDAY	1 Samuel 2:18-20, 26	*Samuel grew in favor with all*
	Psalm 148	*God's splendor over the earth*
	Colossians 3:12-17	*Clothe yourselves in love*
	Luke 2:41-52	*Jesus increased in favor with all*

MONDAY	1 Chronicles 28:1-10	*Solomon will build the temple*
TUESDAY	2 Chronicles 7:1-11	*Solomon dedicates the temple*
WEDNESDAY	Luke 8:16-21	*Jesus' family*
THURSDAY	Ezekiel 43:1-12	*God's glory in the temple*
FRIDAY	Hebrews 9:1-14	*The temple of Christ, the high priest*
SATURDAY	Psalm 11	*God is in the temple*

Second Sunday after Christmas

SUNDAY	Jeremiah 31:7-14	*Joy as God's scattered flock gathers*
	Psalm 147:12-20	*Praising God in Zion*
	or Sirach 24:1-12	*Wisdom lives among God's people*
	Wisdom 10:15-21	*Praising the holy name*
	Ephesians 1:3-14	*The will of God made known in Christ*
	John 1:[1-9] 10-18	*God with us*

Epiphany

The Epiphany of Our Lord

JANUARY 6	Isaiah 60:1-6	*Nations come to the light*
	Psalm 72:1-7, 10-14	*All shall bow down*
	Ephesians 3:1-12	*The gospel's promise for all*
	Matthew 2:1-12	*Christ revealed to the nations*

JANUARY 7	Daniel 2:1-19	*The king searches for wisdom*
JANUARY 8	Daniel 2:24-49	*Daniel reveals the dream's meaning*
JANUARY 9	Luke 1:67-79	*The Savior is seen*
JANUARY 10	Numbers 24:15-19	*A star coming from out of Jacob*
JANUARY 11	Ephesians 4:17—5:1	*Life lived in Christ*
JANUARY 12	Daniel 2:20-23	*Praise God's wisdom revealed*

The Baptism of Our Lord

SUNDAY	Isaiah 43:1-7	*Passing through the waters*
	Psalm 29	*The voice of the LORD upon the waters*
	Acts 8:14-17	*Prayer for the Holy Spirit*
	Luke 3:15-17, 21-22	*The baptism of Jesus*
MONDAY	Judges 4:1-10, 12-16	*Israel's enemies drown*
TUESDAY	Judges 5:12-21	*The song of Deborah*
WEDNESDAY	Luke 11:33-36	*Your body full of light*
THURSDAY	Numbers 27:1-11	*Daughters also promised inheritance*
FRIDAY	1 John 5:13-21	*The life of those born of God*
SATURDAY	Psalm 106:1-12	*God saves through water*

Second Sunday after the Epiphany

SUNDAY	Isaiah 62:1-5	*God like the bridegroom and bride*
	Psalm 36:5-10	*We feast on the abundance of God's house*
	1 Corinthians 12:1-11	*A variety of gifts but one Spirit*
	John 2:1-11	*The wedding at Cana*
MONDAY	Isaiah 54:1-8	*God is married to Israel*
TUESDAY	Jeremiah 3:19-25	*Israel is a faithless spouse*
WEDNESDAY	Luke 5:33-39	*Christ the bridegroom*
THURSDAY	Song of Solomon 4:9—5:1	*A love song*
FRIDAY	1 Corinthians 1:3-17	*Appeal for unity*
SATURDAY	Psalm 145	*Praise God's faithfulness*

Third Sunday after the Epiphany

SUNDAY	Nehemiah 8:1-3, 5-6, 8-10	*Ezra reads the law*
	Psalm 19	*The law revives the soul*
	1 Corinthians 12:12-31a	*You are the body of Christ*
	Luke 4:14-21	*Jesus reads the prophet Isaiah*
MONDAY	Jeremiah 36:1-4, 20-26	*The king burns the scroll*
TUESDAY	Jeremiah 36:27-32	*Jeremiah dictates a second scroll*
WEDNESDAY	Luke 4:38-44	*Jesus heals and preaches in synagogues*
THURSDAY	Isaiah 61:1-7	*The spirit of God upon me*
FRIDAY	1 Corinthians 14:1-12	*The assembly's gifts*
SATURDAY	Psalm 119:89-96	*The law of God gives life*

Fourth Sunday after the Epiphany

SUNDAY	Jeremiah 1:4-10	*A prophet to the nations*
	Psalm 71:1-6	*You have been my strength*
	1 Corinthians 13:1-13	*Without love, a noisy gong*
	Luke 4:21-30	*The prophet Jesus not accepted*
MONDAY	1 Kings 17:8-16	*The widow of Zeraphath fed*
TUESDAY	2 Kings 5:1-14	*Naaman the Syrian healed*
WEDNESDAY	Luke 19:41-44	*Recognizing the works of God*
THURSDAY	Jeremiah 1:11-19	*Jeremiah warns of disaster*
FRIDAY	1 Corinthians 14:13-25	*Interpreting tongues*
SATURDAY	Psalm 56	*In God I trust*

Fifth Sunday after the Epiphany

SUNDAY	Isaiah 6:1-8 [9-13]	*Send me*
	Psalm 138	*I will bow toward your holy temple*
	1 Corinthians 15:1-11	*I am the least of the apostles*
	Luke 5:1-11	*Jesus calls the disciples to fish for people*
MONDAY	Numbers 27:12-23	*God's choice of Joshua*
TUESDAY	1 Samuel 9:15—10:1b	*The call of Saul*
WEDNESDAY	Luke 5:27-32	*The call of Levi*
THURSDAY	Isaiah 8:1-15	*Resisting the call*
FRIDAY	1 Corinthians 14:26-40	*Advice about worship*
SATURDAY	Psalm 115	*God blesses the chosen people*

Sixth Sunday after the Epiphany

SUNDAY	Jeremiah 17:5-10	*Those who trust the LORD are like trees*
	Psalm 1	*Trees planted by streams of water*
	1 Corinthians 15:12-20	*Christ has been raised*
	Luke 6:17-26	*Blessings on the poor, woes on the rich*
MONDAY	2 Kings 24:18—25:21	*Woes come upon Jerusalem*
TUESDAY	Ezra 1:1-11	*Blessings return to Jerusalem*
WEDNESDAY	Luke 11:37-52	*Woe to the sinners*
THURSDAY	Jeremiah 22:11-17	*Woe to the unjust*
FRIDAY	1 Corinthians 15:20-34	*The end time*
SATURDAY	Psalm 120	*Woe to me*

Seventh Sunday after the Epiphany

SUNDAY	Genesis 45:3-11, 15	*Joseph forgives his brothers*
	Psalm 37:1-11, 39-40	*The lowly shall possess the land*
	1 Corinthians 15:35-38, 42-50	*The mystery of the resurrection*
	Luke 6:27-38	*Love your enemies*
MONDAY	Genesis 33:1-17	*Jacob and Esau reconcile*
TUESDAY	1 Samuel 24:1-22	*David spares Saul's life*
WEDNESDAY	Luke 17:1-4	*Forgiving seven times seven*
THURSDAY	Leviticus 5:1-13	*Offerings for pardon*
FRIDAY	1 Corinthians 11:2-22, 27-33	*Advice for church life*
SATURDAY	Psalm 38	*Confession of sin*

Eighth Sunday after the Epiphany

SUNDAY	Isaiah 55:10-13	*God's word goes forth*
	Psalm 92:1-4, 12-15	*The righteous flourish like a palm tree*
	or Sirach 27:4-7	*Wisdom rules heaven and earth*
	1 Corinthians 15:51-58	*The mystery of the resurrection*
	Luke 6:39-49	*Building on a firm foundation*
MONDAY	Jeremiah 24:1-10	*The good figs and the bad figs*
TUESDAY	Jeremiah 29:10-19	*The rotten figs*
WEDNESDAY	Luke 14:34-35	*Good or bad salt*
THURSDAY	Proverbs 5:1-23	*The poem of the bad woman or the good wife*
FRIDAY	1 Corinthians 16:1-24	*Paul's farewell*
SATURDAY	Psalm 1	*The fruited tree or the chaff*

The Transfiguration of Our Lord

SUNDAY	Exodus 34:29-35	*Moses' face shone*
	Psalm 99	*Worship upon God's holy hill*
	2 Corinthians 3:12—4:2	*We will be transformed*
	Luke 9:28-36 [37-43]	*Jesus is transfigured on the mountain*
MONDAY	Ezekiel 1:1—2:1	*Ezekiel's vision of the chariot*
TUESDAY	Luke 10:21-24	*The Son revealed*

Lent

Ash Wednesday

	Joel 2:1-2, 12-17	*Return to God*
	or Isaiah 58:1-12	*The fast that God chooses*
	Psalm 51:1-17	*A plea for mercy*
	2 Corinthians 5:20b—6:10	*Now is the day of salvation*
	Matthew 6:1-6, 16-21	*The practice of faith*
THURSDAY	Exodus 5:10-23	*Israel labors in Egypt*
FRIDAY	Exodus 6:1-13	*God promises deliverance*
SATURDAY	Ecclesiastes 3:1-8	*For everything a season*

First Sunday in Lent

SUNDAY	Deuteronomy 26:1-11	*Saved from Egypt*
	Psalm 91:1-2, 9-16	*God shall keep you*
	Romans 10:8b-13	*You will be saved*
	Luke 4:1-13	*The temptation of Jesus*
MONDAY	1 Chronicles 21:1-17	*Satan tempts David*
TUESDAY	Zechariah 3:1-10	*Satan tempts Joshua*
WEDNESDAY	Luke 21:34—22:6	*Satan enters Judas*
THURSDAY	Job 1:1-22	*Satan tempts Job*
FRIDAY	2 Peter 2:4-21	*Believers who fall into sin*
SATURDAY	Psalm 17	*Prayer for protection from evil ones*

Second Sunday in Lent

SUNDAY	Genesis 15:1-12, 17-18	*The covenant with Abram*
	Psalm 27	*The LORD shall keep me safe*
	Philippians 3:17—4:1	*Our citizenship is in heaven*
	Luke 13:31-35	*A hen gathering her brood*
MONDAY	Exodus 33:1-6	*Abraham's descendants lament*
TUESDAY	Numbers 14:10b-24	*Moses intercedes for the people*
WEDNESDAY	Luke 13:22-31	*The narrow door*
THURSDAY	2 Chronicles 20:1-22	*The king prays for Jerusalem*
FRIDAY	Romans 4:1-12	*The faith of Abraham*
SATURDAY	Psalm 105:1-15 [16-41] 42	*God's covenant with Abraham*

Third Sunday in Lent

SUNDAY	Isaiah 55:1-9	*Come to the water*
	Psalm 63:1-8	*O God, eagerly I seek you*
	1 Corinthians 10:1-13	*Israel, baptized in cloud and seas*
	Luke 13:1-9	*The parable of the fig tree*
MONDAY	Jeremiah 11:1-17	*Judgment against the olive tree*
TUESDAY	Ezekiel 17:1-10	*Allegory of the vine*
WEDNESDAY	Luke 13:18-21	*Parables of the mustard seed, yeast*
THURSDAY	Numbers 13:17-27	*The fruit of the promised land*
FRIDAY	Romans 2:1-16	*Divine judgment*
SATURDAY	Psalm 39	*My hope is in God*

Fourth Sunday in Lent

SUNDAY	Joshua 5:9-12	*Israel eats bread and grain*
	Psalm 32	*Be glad, you righteous*
	2 Corinthians 5:16-21	*The mystery and ministry of reconciliation*
	Luke 15:1-3, 11b-32	*The parable of the forgiving father*
MONDAY	Leviticus 23:26-41	*Days for confession and celebration*
TUESDAY	Leviticus 25:1-19	*The jubilee celebration*
WEDNESDAY	Luke 9:10-17	*Jesus feeds 5000*
THURSDAY	2 Kings 4:1-7	*The widow saved*
FRIDAY	Revelation 19:1-9	*The marriage supper of the Lamb*
SATURDAY	Psalm 53	*Restoring our fortunes*

Fifth Sunday in Lent

SUNDAY	Isaiah 43:16-21	*The LORD gives water in the wilderness*
	Psalm 126	*Sowing with tears, reaping with joy*
	Philippians 3:4b-14	*To know Christ and his resurrection*
	John 12:1-8	*Mary anoints Jesus for his burial*
MONDAY	Exodus 40:1-15	*Anointing the holy things*
TUESDAY	Judges 9:7-15	*Anointing the bramble*
WEDNESDAY	Luke 18:31-34	*Jesus foretells his death*
THURSDAY	Habakkuk 3:2-15	*God will save the anointed*
FRIDAY	1 John 2:18-28	*Knowing the Son*
SATURDAY	Psalm 20	*The Anointed One and us*

Sunday of the Passion

PALM SUNDAY	Luke 19:28-40	*Entrance into the final days*
	Psalm 118:1-2, 19-29	*Blessed is the one who comes*
	Isaiah 50:4-9a	*The servant submits to suffering*
	Psalm 31:9-16	*I commend my spirit*
	Philippians 2:5-11	*Humbled to the point of death*
	Luke 22:14—23:56	*The passion and death of Jesus*
MONDAY	Genesis 34:1-31	*Violence against Dinah and Shechem*
TUESDAY	Judges 19:22-30	*Violence against the Levite's concubine*
WEDNESDAY	2 Samuel 13:1-22	*Violence against Tamar*

The Three Days

Maundy Thursday

	Exodus 12:1-4 [5-10] 11-14	*The passover of the LORD*
	Psalm 116:1-2, 12-19	*The cup of salvation*
	1 Corinthians 11:23-26	*Proclaim the Lord's death until he comes*
	John 13:1-17, 31b-35	*The service of Christ: footwashing and meal*

Good Friday

	Isaiah 52:13—53:12	*The suffering servant*
	Psalm 22	*My God, why have you forsaken me?*
	Hebrews 10:16-25	*The way to God is opened*
	or Hebrews 4:14-16; 5:7-9	*Jesus, the merciful high priest*
	John 18:1—19:42	*The passion and death of Jesus*

Holy Saturday

	1 Samuel 4:1b-11	*The ark of God captured*

The Resurrection of Our Lord | Vigil of Easter

READINGS AND RESPONSES	Genesis 1:1—2:4a	*Creation*
	Psalm 136:1-9, 23-36	*God's mercy endures forever*
	Genesis 7:1-5,11-18; 8:6-18; 9:8-13	*The flood*
	Psalm 46	*The God of Jacob is our stronghold*
	Genesis 22:1-18	*The testing of Abraham*
	Psalm 16	*You will show me the path of life*
	Exodus 14:10-31; 15:20-21	*Israel's deliverance at the Red Sea*
	Exodus 15:1b-13, 17-18	*The LORD has triumphed gloriously*
	Isaiah 55:1-11	*Salvation freely offered to all*
	Isaiah 12:2-6	*The wells of salvation*
	Proverbs 8:1-8, 19-21; 9:4b-6	
	or Baruch 3:9-15, 32—4:4	*The wisdom of God*
	Psalm 19	*The law is just and rejoices in the heart*
	Ezekiel 36:24-28	*A new heart and a new spirit*
	Psalm 42 and Psalm 43	*My soul thirsts for the living God*
	Ezekiel 37:1-14	*The valley of the dry bones*
	Psalm 143	*Revive me, O LORD*
	Zephaniah 3:14-20	*The gathering of God's people*
	Psalm 98	*Lift up your voice, rejoice and sing*
	Jonah 3:1-10	*The call of Jonah*
	Jonah 2:1-3 [4-6] 7-9	*Deliverance belongs to the LORD*
	Deuteronomy 31:19-30	*The song of Moses*
	Deuteronomy 32:1-4, 7, 36a, 43a	*Justice for the people*
	Daniel 3:1-29	*The fiery furnace*
	Song of the Three Young Men 3:35-65	*Sing praise to the LORD*
	Romans 6:3-11	*Dying and rising with Christ*
	Psalm 114	*Tremble, O earth*
	Luke 24:1-12	*He is risen*

Easter

The Resurrection of Our Lord | Easter Day

SUNDAY	Acts 10:34-43	*God raised Jesus on the third day*
	or Isaiah 65:17-25	*God promises a new heaven and a new earth*
	Psalm 118:1-2, 14-24	*On this day the LORD has acted*
	1 Corinthians 15:19-26	*Christ raised from the dead*
	or Acts 10:34-43	*God raised Jesus on the third day*
	John 20:1-18	*Seeing the risen Christ*
	or Luke 24:1-12	*The women proclaim the resurrection*

The Resurrection of Our Lord | Easter Evening

SUNDAY	Isaiah 25:6-9	*The feast of victory*
	Psalm 114	*Hallelujah*
	1 Corinthians 5:6b-8	*Celebrating with sincerity and truth*
	Luke 24:13-49	*At evening, the risen Christ is revealed*
MONDAY	Joshua 10:16-27	*Joshua defeats five kings*
TUESDAY	2 Samuel 6:1-15	*David dances before the ark*
WEDNESDAY	Luke 24:1-12	*The resurrection according to Luke*
THURSDAY	Judges 4:17-23; 5:24-31a	*Jael kills Sisera*
FRIDAY	Revelation 12:1-12	*The woman, the child, the dragon*
SATURDAY	Psalm 108	*God saves the chosen people*

Second Sunday of Easter

SUNDAY	Acts 5:27-32	*The God of our ancestors raised up Jesus*
	Psalm 118:14-29	*Glad songs of victory*
	or Psalm 150	*Let everything praise the LORD*
	Revelation 1:4-8	*Jesus Christ, the firstborn of the dead*
	John 20:19-31	*Beholding the wounds of the risen Christ*
MONDAY	1 Samuel 17:1-23	*The enemy Goliath taunts Israel*
TUESDAY	1 Samuel 17:32-51	*David conquers Goliath*
WEDNESDAY	Luke 12:4-12	*The courage to confess Christ*
THURSDAY	Esther 9:1-5, 18-23	*Purim celebrates victory*
FRIDAY	Revelation 1:9-18	*A vision of Christ*
SATURDAY	Psalm 122	*Peace in Jerusalem*

Third Sunday of Easter

SUNDAY	Acts 9:1-6 [7-20]	*Paul's conversion, baptism, and preaching*
	Psalm 30	*My wailing turns into dancing*
	Revelation 5:11-14	*The song of the living creatures to the Lamb*
	John 21:1-19	*Jesus appears to the disciples*
MONDAY	Acts 12:1-19	*Peter imprisoned*
TUESDAY	Acts 26:1, 12-29	*Paul preaches before Agrippa*
WEDNESDAY	Luke 5:1-11	*Simon's catch of fish*
THURSDAY	Acts 11:19-30	*The early Christian community*
FRIDAY	Revelation 5:1-10	*The throne and the elders*
SATURDAY	Psalm 121	*God will preserve your life*

Fourth Sunday of Easter

SUNDAY	Acts 9:36-43	*Peter raises Tabitha from the dead*
	Psalm 23	*The LORD is my shepherd*
	Revelation 7:9-17	*A multitude sings before the Lamb*
	John 10:22-30	*Jesus promises life to his sheep*
MONDAY	Ezekiel 37:15-28	*God will unite the flock*
TUESDAY	Ezekiel 45:1-9	*God promises a sanctuary*
WEDNESDAY	John 10:31-42	*The Son and the Father are one*
THURSDAY	Jeremiah 50:17-20	*Israel will be fed*
FRIDAY	Revelation 6:1—7:3	*Israel sealed*
SATURDAY	Psalm 100	*We are God's sheep*

Fifth Sunday of Easter

SUNDAY	Acts 11:1-18	*God saves the Gentiles*
	Psalm 148	*God's splendor is over earth and heaven*
	Revelation 21:1-6	*New heaven, new earth*
	John 13:31-35	*Love one another*
MONDAY	1 Samuel 20:1-23, 35-42	*The love of David and Jonathan*
TUESDAY	2 Samuel 1:4-27	*David mourns Jonathan's death*
WEDNESDAY	Luke 10:25-28	*Love your neighbor*
THURSDAY	Leviticus 19:9-18	*Love your neighbor*
FRIDAY	Revelation 10:1-11	*Eating the scroll*
SATURDAY	Psalm 133	*How good it is to live in unity*

Sixth Sunday of Easter

SUNDAY	Acts 16:9-15	*Lydia and her household are baptized*
	Psalm 67	*Let the nations be glad*
	Revelation 21:10, 22—22:5	*The Lamb is the light of God's city*
	John 14:23-29	*The Father will send the Holy Spirit*
	or John 5:1-9	*Jesus heals on the sabbath*
MONDAY	1 Chronicles 12:16-22	*The spirit of God on Amasai*
TUESDAY	2 Chronicles 15:1-15	*The spirit of God on Azariah*
WEDNESDAY	Luke 2:25-38	*The Spirit of God on Simeon and Anna*

The Ascension of Our Lord

	Acts 1:1-11	*Jesus sends the apostles*
	Psalm 47	*God has gone up with a shout*
	or Psalm 93	*God's throne has been established*
	Ephesians 1:15-23	*Seeing the risen and ascended Christ*
	Luke 24:44-53	*Christ present in all times and places*
FRIDAY	Revelation 12:13-17	*The dragon makes war*
SATURDAY	Psalm 125	*The peace of God*

Seventh Sunday of Easter

SUNDAY	Acts 16:16-34	*A jailer is baptized*
	Psalm 97	*Light dawns for the righteous*
	Revelation 22:12-14, 16-17, 20-21	*Blessed are those who wash their robes*
	John 17:20-26	*Jesus prays for the disciples*
MONDAY	Exodus 40:16-38	*God's glory on the tabernacle*
TUESDAY	2 Chronicles 5:2-14	*God's glory in the temple*
WEDNESDAY	Luke 9:18-27	*God's glory and discipleship*
THURSDAY	Ezekiel 3:12-21	*God's glory commissions the prophet*
FRIDAY	Revelation 19:9-21	*The rider and the beast*
SATURDAY	Psalm 29	*The glory of God*

Vigil of Pentecost

	Exodus 19:1-9	*The covenant at Sinai*
	or Acts 2:1-11	*Filled with the Spirit to tell God's deeds*
	Psalm 33:12-22	*The LORD, our help and our shield*
	or Psalm 130	*There is forgiveness with you*
	Romans 8:14-17, 22-27	*Praying with the Spirit*
	John 7:37-39	*Jesus, the true living water*

The Day of Pentecost

SUNDAY	Acts 2:1-21	*Filled with the Spirit*
	or Genesis 11:1-9	*God destroys the tower of Babel*
	Psalm 104:24-34, 35b	*Send forth your spirit*
	Romans 8:14-17	*The Spirit makes us children of God*
	or Acts 2:1-21	*Filled with the Spirit*
	John 14:8-17 [25-27]	*The Father will give you the Spirit of truth*
MONDAY	Joel 2:18-29	*God's spirit poured out*
TUESDAY	Ezekiel 11:14-25	*God will gather the people*
WEDNESDAY	Luke 1:26-38	*God's Spirit comes on Mary*
THURSDAY	Numbers 24:1-14	*Balaam speaks with God's spirit*
FRIDAY	1 Corinthians 2:1-13	*About the Spirit of God*
SATURDAY	Psalm 48	*The God of Zion*

The Holy Trinity

SUNDAY	Proverbs 8:1-4, 22-31	*Wisdom rejoices in the creation*
	Psalm 8	*Your majesty is praised above the heavens*
	Romans 5:1-5	*God's love poured into our hearts*
	John 16:12-15	*The Spirit will guide you into the truth*
MONDAY	Proverbs 3:13-26	*Wisdom is a tree of life*
TUESDAY	Proverbs 4:1-9	*Choose God's wisdom*
WEDNESDAY	Luke 1:46-55	*Mary sings of God*
THURSDAY	Daniel 1:1-21	*Daniel's wisdom*
FRIDAY	Ephesians 4:1-16	*Life in the Trinity*
SATURDAY	Psalm 124	*We have escaped like a bird*

Sunday between May 24 and 28 (Proper 3)

SUNDAY	Isaiah 55:10-13	*God's word goes forth*
	or Sirach 27:4-7	*Wisdom rules heaven and earth*
	Psalm 92:1-4, 11-14	*The righteous flourish like a palm tree*
	1 Corinthians 14:41-58	*The mystery of the resurrection*
	Luke 6:39-49	*Building on a firm foundation*

Sunday between May 29 and June 4 inclusive (Proper 4)

SUNDAY	1 Kings 8:22-23, 41-43	*God's everlasting covenant for all*
	Psalm 96:1-9	*Praise to God among the nations*
	or 1 Kings 18:20-21 [22-29]	
	30-39	*Elijah and the prophets of Baal*
	Psalm 96	*Give glory to God's name*
	Galatians 1:1-12	*Beware of contrary gospels*
	Luke 7:1-10	*Jesus heals the centurion's slave*
MONDAY	Jonah 4:1-11	*God's mercy on the Ninevites*
TUESDAY	Nehemiah 1:1-11	*Prayer for God to gather the people*
WEDNESDAY	Luke 4:31-37	*Healing the man with an unclean spirit*
THURSDAY	Isaiah 56:1-8	*God welcomes the foreigner and eunuch*
FRIDAY	Acts 3:1-10	*Healing the crippled beggar*
SATURDAY	Psalm 5	*God's favor like a shield*

Sunday between June 5 and 11 inclusive (Proper 5)

SUNDAY	1 Kings 17:17-24	*Elijah revives a widow's son*
	Psalm 30	*My God, you restored me to health*
	or 1 Kings 17:8-16 [17-24]	*A widow offers hospitality to Elijah*
	Psalm 146	*The LORD lifts those bowed down*
	Galatians 1:11-24	*Jesus Christ is revealed*
	Luke 7:11-17	*Jesus revives a widow's son*
MONDAY	Genesis 22:1-14	*God saves Isaac from death*
TUESDAY	Judges 11:29-40	*God does not save Jephthah's daughter*
WEDNESDAY	Luke 8:40-56	*A girl raised to life, a woman healed*
THURSDAY	Jeremiah 8:14-22	*A balm in Gilead*
FRIDAY	Galatians 2:1-14	*Paul and Peter*
SATURDAY	Psalm 68:1-10, 19-20	*God protects the widows*

Sunday between June 12 and 18 inclusive (Proper 6)

SUNDAY	2 Samuel 11:26—12:10, 13-15	*Nathan tells the story of the lamb*
	Psalm 32	*You forgive the guilt of my sin*
	or 1 Kings 21:1-10 [11-14] 15-21	*Ahab kills the owner of a vineyard*
	Psalm 5:1-8	*Trust in God for deliverance*
	Galatians 2:15-21	*Justification through grace*
	Luke 7:36—8:3	*The woman anointing Jesus is forgiven*
MONDAY	2 Chronicles 30:1-12	*The people ask for forgiveness*
TUESDAY	2 Chronicles 30:13-27	*The people are forgiven*
WEDNESDAY	Luke 5:17-26	*Jesus forgives sins and heals*
THURSDAY	2 Samuel 18:28—19:8	*David forgives Absalom*
FRIDAY	Galatians 3:1-14	*Abraham believed God*
SATURDAY	Psalm 130	*Prayer for mercy*

Sunday between June 19 and 25 inclusive (Proper 7)

SUNDAY	Isaiah 65:1-9	*The prophet sent to a rebellious people*
	Psalm 22:19-28	*I will praise you*
	or 1 Kings 19:1-4 [5-7] 8-15a	*Elijah hears God in silence*
	Psalm 42 and Psalm 43	*Send out your light and truth*
	Galatians 3:23-29	*Clothed with Christ in baptism*
	Luke 8:26-39	*Jesus casts out demons*
MONDAY	Job 18:1-21	*God will destroy the wicked*
TUESDAY	Job 19:1-22	*Job questions God's ways*
WEDNESDAY	Luke 9:37-43	*Jesus heals the boy with a demon*
THURSDAY	Ezekiel 32:1-10	*Evil like a dragon will be destroyed*
FRIDAY	Galatians 3:15-22	*The purpose of the law*
SATURDAY	Psalm 64	*Prayer for protection*

Sunday between June 26 and July 2 inclusive (Proper 8)

SUNDAY	1 Kings 19:15-16, 19-21	*Elijah says, Follow me*
	Psalm 16	*Protect me, O God*
	or 2 Kings 2:1-2, 6-14	*Elijah ascends into heaven*
	Psalm 77:1-2, 11-20	*You have redeemed your people*
	Galatians 5:1, 13-25	*Love is the whole of the law*
	Luke 9:51-62	*Jesus says, Follow me*
MONDAY	Leviticus 9:22—10:11	*God's fire consumes Aaron's sons*
TUESDAY	2 Kings 1:1-16	*God's fire consumes the king's men*
WEDNESDAY	Luke 9:21-27	*Following Jesus*
THURSDAY	Deuteronomy 32:15-27, 39-43	*God's anger like a fire*
FRIDAY	Galatians 4:8-20	*Paul reproves the hearers*
SATURDAY	Psalm 140	*Prayer for protection*

Sunday between July 3 and 9 inclusive (Proper 9)

SUNDAY	Isaiah 66:10-14	*Jerusalem, a nursing mother*
	Psalm 66:1-9	*God holds our souls in life*
	or 2 Kings 5:1-14	*Elisha heals a warrior with leprosy*
	Psalm 30	*My God, I cried out to you for help*
	Galatians 6:[1-6] 7-16	*Do what is right now*
	Luke 10:1-11, 16-20	*Jesus sends out seventy disciples*
MONDAY	Jeremiah 6:10-19	*Call to faithfulness*
TUESDAY	Jeremiah 8:4-13	*Call to faithfulness*
WEDNESDAY	Luke 9:1-6	*The mission of the Twelve*
THURSDAY	Joshua 23:1-16	*Joshua urges faithfulness*
FRIDAY	Acts 19:21-41	*A riot from Paul's preaching*
SATURDAY	Psalm 119:73-80	*Living in faithfulness*

Sunday between July 10 and 16 inclusive (Proper 10)

SUNDAY	Deuteronomy 30:9-14	*The LORD delights in your fruitfulness*
	Psalm 25:1-10	*Show me your ways*
	or Amos 7:7-17	*A plumb line judging the people*
	Psalm 82	*O God, rule the earth*
	Colossians 1:1-14	*The gospel is bearing fruit*
	Luke 10:25-37	*The parable of the merciful Samaritan*
MONDAY	Genesis 41:14-36	*Joseph's plan to feed Egypt*
TUESDAY	Genesis 41:37-49	*God saves Egypt from starvation*
WEDNESDAY	John 3:16-21	*God's Son saves the world*
THURSDAY	Leviticus 19:1-4, 32-37	*Mercy to the alien*
FRIDAY	James 2:14-26	*Faith produces good works*
SATURDAY	Psalm 25	*Teach me your paths*

Sunday between July 17 and 23 inclusive (Proper 11)

SUNDAY	Genesis 18:1-10a	*The hospitality of Abraham and Sarah*
	Psalm 15	*Leading a blameless life*
	or Amos 8:1-12	*A famine of hearing God's words*
	Psalm 52	*I am like a green olive tree*
	Colossians 1:15-28	*A hymn to Christ*
	Luke 10:38-42	*Choosing the better part*
MONDAY	Exodus 18:1-12	*Jethro's family eats before God*
TUESDAY	Proverbs 9:1-18	*The wise and the foolish women*
WEDNESDAY	Luke 8:4-10	*Jesus speaks in parables*
THURSDAY	Deuteronomy 12:1-12	*The promise to eat before God*
FRIDAY	Colossians 1:27—2:7	*To know Christ*
SATURDAY	Psalm 119:97-104	*God's word like honey*

Sunday between July 24 and 30 inclusive (Proper 12)

SUNDAY	Genesis 18:20-32	*Abraham bargains with God*
	Psalm 138	*Your love endures forever*
	or Hosea 1:2-10	*Hosea's marriage*
	Psalm 85	*Righteousness and peace*
	Colossians 2:6-15 [16-19]	*Buried with Christ in baptism*
	Luke 11:1-13	*Jesus teaches prayer*
MONDAY	Esther 3:7-15	*Haman's plot to kill the Jews*
TUESDAY	Esther 7:1-10	*Esther's plea saves the Jews*
WEDNESDAY	Luke 8:22-25	*Disciples pray for safety*
THURSDAY	Job 22:21—23:17	*Eliphaz and Job argue about prayer*
FRIDAY	Colossians 2:16—3:1	*About false regulations*
SATURDAY	Psalm 55:16-23	*Cast your burden on God*

Sunday between July 31 and August 6 inclusive (Proper 13)

SUNDAY	Ecclesiastes 1:2, 12-14; 2:18-23	*Search out wisdom*
	Psalm 49:1-12	*The folly of trust in riches*
	or Hosea 11:1-11	*Like a mother, God loves Israel*
	Psalm 107:1-9, 43	*Give thanks to the Most High*
	Colossians 3:1-11	*Clothed in Christ*
	Luke 12:13-21	*Be rich toward God, your treasure*
MONDAY	Ecclesiastes 2:1-17	*The fool accumulates wealth*
TUESDAY	Ecclesiastes 3:16—4:8	*Death comes to all*
WEDNESDAY	Luke 12:22-31	*Trust in God*
THURSDAY	Ecclesiastes 12:1-8, 13-14	*Remember God*
FRIDAY	Colossians 3:18—4:5	*A household code*
SATURDAY	Psalm 127	*The foolish life, the righteous life*

Sunday between August 7 and 13 inclusive (Proper 14)

SUNDAY	Genesis 15:1-6	*God's promise of a child*
	Psalm 33:12-22	*Let your lovingkindness be upon us*
	or Isaiah 1:1, 10-20	*Learn to do good*
	Psalm 50:1-8, 22-23	*The salvation of God*
	Hebrews 11:1-3, 8-16	*Abraham's faith in a home given by God*
	Luke 12:32-40	*The treasure of the kingdom*
MONDAY	2 Chronicles 33:1-17	*Manasseh returns to God*
TUESDAY	2 Chronicles 34:22-33	*Huldah preaches the covenant*
WEDNESDAY	Luke 12:41-48	*A parable of the slaves*
THURSDAY	Jeremiah 33:14-26	*God remembers the covenant with David*
FRIDAY	Hebrews 11:1-7, 17-28	*The ancestors' faith*
SATURDAY	Psalm 89:1-18	*God's covenant with David*

Sunday between August 14 and 20 inclusive (Proper 15)

SUNDAY	Jeremiah 23:23-29	*God's word is like fire*
	Psalm 82	*O God, rule the earth*
	or Isaiah 5:1-7	*The vineyard of the LORD is destroyed*
	Psalm 80:1-2, 8-19	*O God, tend this vine*
	Hebrews 11:29—12:2	*The faith of the Hebrew people*
	Luke 12:49-56	*Jesus brings fire on earth*
MONDAY	1 Samuel 5:1-12	*The Philistines punished with plague*
TUESDAY	1 Samuel 6:1-16	*The Philistines atone for sacrilege*
WEDNESDAY	Luke 19:45-48	*Jesus cleanses the temple*
THURSDAY	Joshua 7:1, 10-26	*Achan punished for disobedience*
FRIDAY	Hebrews 10:26-39	*God's judgment*
SATURDAY	Psalm 32	*Prayer for forgiveness*

Sunday between August 21 and 27 inclusive (Proper 16)

SUNDAY	Isaiah 58:9b-14	*Do not trample the sabbath*
	Psalm 103:1-8	*Crowned with mercy and lovingkindness*
	or Jeremiah 1:4-10	*Jeremiah called to be a prophet*
	Psalm 71:1-6	*You have been my strength*
	Hebrews 12:18-29	*Coming to the city of the living God*
	Luke 13:10-17	*Jesus heals on the sabbath*
MONDAY	Nehemiah 13:15-22	*Nehemiah enforces sabbath law*
TUESDAY	Ezekiel 20:1-17	*The people profaned the sabbath*
WEDNESDAY	Luke 6:1-11	*Jesus heals on the sabbath*
THURSDAY	Acts 17:1-9	*Paul preaches Christ on the sabbath*
FRIDAY	Hebrews 12:3-17	*Call for endurance*
SATURDAY	Psalm 109:21-31	*Praise for healing*

Sunday between Aug. 28 and Sept. 3 inclusive (Proper 17)

SUNDAY	Proverbs 25:6-7	*Do not put yourself forward*
	or Sirach 10:12-18	*Judgment upon the proud*
	Psalm 112	*The righteous are merciful*
	or Jeremiah 2:4-13	*The people of Israel forsake the LORD*
	Psalm 81:1, 10-16	*Honey from the rock*
	Hebrews 13:1-8, 15-16	*God is with us*
	Luke 14:1, 7-14	*Invite the poor to your banquet*
MONDAY	Isaiah 2:5-17	*God condemns the proud*
TUESDAY	Isaiah 57:14-21	*God blesses the humble*
WEDNESDAY	Luke 14:15-24	*God's hospitality to the humble*
THURSDAY	2 Chronicles 12:1-12	*King Rehoboam humbles himself*
FRIDAY	Hebrews 13:7-21	*Call for faithfulness*
SATURDAY	Psalm 119:65-72	*God blesses the humble*

Sunday between September 4 and 10 inclusive (Proper 18)

SUNDAY	Deuteronomy 30:15-20	*Walk in the way of life*
	Psalm 1	*Delight in the law*
	or Jeremiah 18:1-11	*Like a potter, the LORD reshapes Israel*
	Psalm 139:1-6, 13-18	*You have searched me out*
	Philemon 1-21	*Paul says, Receive Onesimus*
	Luke 14:25-33	*Give up your possessions*
MONDAY	Genesis 39:1-23	*Joseph does not sin against God*
TUESDAY	2 Kings 17:24-41	*The Assyrians worship other gods*
WEDNESDAY	Luke 18:18-30	*The rich ruler*
THURSDAY	Deuteronomy 7:12-26	*The way of obedience*
FRIDAY	1 Timothy 3:14—4:16	*Being a servant of Christ*
SATURDAY	Psalm 101	*Choosing God's law*

Sunday between September 11 and 17 inclusive (Proper 19)

SUNDAY	Exodus 32:7-14	*Moses begs forgiveness*
	Psalm 51:1-10	*Have mercy on me, O God*
	or Jeremiah 4:11-12, 22-28	*Judgment against Jerusalem*
	Psalm 14	*Who seeks after God?*
	1 Timothy 1:12-17	*Christ Jesus came for sinners*
	Luke 15:1-10	*Looking for the lost sheep and silver coin*
MONDAY	Amos 7:1-6	*God relents from punishing Israel*
TUESDAY	Jonah 3:1-10	*God relents from punishing Nineveh*
WEDNESDAY	Luke 22:31-33, 54-62	*Peter denies Jesus*
THURSDAY	Job 40:6-14; 42:1-6	*Job repents*
FRIDAY	1 Timothy 1:1-11	*About false teachers*
SATURDAY	Psalm 73	*God is my portion*

Sunday between September 18 and 24 inclusive (Proper 20)

SUNDAY	Amos 8:4-7	*Warnings to those who trample the needy*
	Psalm 113	*Our God lifts up the poor*
	or Jeremiah 8:18—9:1	*The LORD laments over Judah*
	Psalm 79:1-9	*Deliver us and forgive us our sins*
	1 Timothy 2:1-7	*One God, one mediator, Christ Jesus*
	Luke 16:1-13	*Serving God or wealth*
MONDAY	Proverbs 14:12-31	*Oppressing the poor*
TUESDAY	Proverbs 17:1-5	*Oppressing the poor*
WEDNESDAY	Luke 20:45—21:4	*The rich versus the poor*
THURSDAY	Exodus 23:1-9	*Justice for all*
FRIDAY	2 Corinthians 8:1-9	*Generosity to the poor*
SATURDAY	Psalm 12	*Help for the poor*

Sunday between Sept. 25 and Oct. 1 inclusive (Proper 21)

SUNDAY	Amos 6:1a, 4-7	*Warnings to the wealthy*
	Psalm 146	*Justice to the oppressed*
	or Jeremiah 32:1-3a, 6-15	*Jeremiah buys a field*
	Psalm 91:1-6, 14-16	*My refuge, my stronghold, my God*
	1 Timothy 6:6-19	*Pursuing God's justice*
	Luke 16:19-31	*Poor Lazarus and the rich man*
MONDAY	Proverbs 22:2-16	*The rich versus the poor*
TUESDAY	Proverbs 28:3-10	*The rich versus the poor*
WEDNESDAY	Luke 9:43b-48	*Welcoming the little ones*
THURSDAY	Ezekiel 18:5-24	*The righteous versus the wicked*
FRIDAY	Revelation 3:14-22	*Being rich or poor in God*
SATURDAY	Psalm 62	*I wait on God*

Sunday between October 2 and 8 inclusive (Proper 22)

SUNDAY	Habakkuk 1:1-4; 2:1-4	*The wicked surround the righteous*
	Psalm 37:1-9	*Commit your way to the LORD*
	or Lamentations 1:1-6	*Jerusalem is empty and destroyed*
	Lamentations 3:19-26	*Great is your faithfulness*
	2 Timothy 1:1-14	*Guard the treasure entrusted to you*
	Luke 17:5-10	*Faith the size of a mustard seed*
MONDAY	2 Kings 18:1-8, 28-36	*King Hezekiah trusts in God*
TUESDAY	2 Kings 19:8-20, 35-37	*God saves the people*
WEDNESDAY	Matthew 20:29-34	*Mercy on the blind man*
THURSDAY	Isaiah 7:1-9	*Standing firm in faith*
FRIDAY	Revelation 2:12-29	*Call to faithfulness*
SATURDAY	Psalm 3	*Deliverance from God*

Sunday between October 9 and 15 inclusive (Proper 23)

SUNDAY	2 Kings 5:1-3, 7-15c	*Naaman is cleansed*
	Psalm 111	*I give thanks with my whole heart*
	or Jeremiah 29:1, 4-7	*Israel plants gardens in Babylon*
	Psalm 66:1-12	*God holds our souls in life*
	2 Timothy 2:8-15	*We will live with Christ*
	Luke 17:11-19	*One leper gives thanks to God*
MONDAY	Numbers 12:1-15	*Miriam contracts leprosy*
TUESDAY	Leviticus 14:33-53	*Cleansing a leprous house*
WEDNESDAY	Luke 5:12-16	*A leper healed*
THURSDAY	Nehemiah 13:1-3, 23-31	*Israel separates from foreigners*
FRIDAY	2 Timothy 2:1-7	*Share in sufferings*
SATURDAY	Psalm 61	*Prayer for health*

Sunday between October 16 and 22 inclusive (Proper 24)

SUNDAY	Genesis 32:22-31	*Jacob's struggle with the angel*
	Psalm 121	*My help comes from the LORD*
	or Jeremiah 31:27-34	*The promise of a new covenant*
	Psalm 119:97-104	*Your words are sweeter than honey*
	2 Timothy 3:14—4:5	*Christ the judge*
	Luke 18:1-8	*A widow begs for justice*
MONDAY	1 Samuel 25:2-22	*David judges against Nabal*
TUESDAY	1 Samuel 25:23-35 [36-42]	*Abigail pleads for life*
WEDNESDAY	Luke 22:39-46	*Jesus prays for life*
THURSDAY	Isaiah 54:11-17	*God will vindicate the faithful*
FRIDAY	2 Timothy 2:14-26	*About the Christian life*
SATURDAY	Psalm 57	*Vindication from God*

Sunday between October 23 and 29 inclusive (Proper 25)

SUNDAY	Jeremiah 14:7-10, 19-22	*Jerusalem will be defeated*
	or Sirach 35:12-17	*God is impartial in justice*
	Psalm 84:1-7	*Happy are the people whose strength is in you*
	or Joel 2:23-32	*The promise to restore Israel*
	Psalm 65	*Your paths overflow with plenty*
	2 Timothy 4:6-8, 16-18	*The good fight of faith*
	Luke 18:9-14	*A Pharisee and tax collector pray*
MONDAY	Daniel 5:1-12	*King Balshazzar sees writing on the wall*
TUESDAY	Daniel 5:13-31	*Daniel urges humility*
WEDNESDAY	Luke 1:46-55	*Mary's song*
THURSDAY	1 Samuel 2:1-10	*Hannah's song*
FRIDAY	2 Timothy 3:1-15	*Godlessness, godliness*
SATURDAY	Psalm 84	*A doorkeeper in God's house*

Sunday between Oct. 30 and Nov. 5 inclusive (Proper 26)

SUNDAY	Isaiah 1:10-18	*Learn to do good*
	Psalm 32:1-7	*Praying in time of trouble*
	or Habakkuk 1:1-4; 2:1-4	*The righteous live by faith*
	Psalm 119:137-144	*Grant me understanding*
	2 Thessalonians 1:1-4, 11-12	*Faith and love amid adversity*
	Luke 19:1-10	*Zacchaeus climbs high to see Jesus*
MONDAY	Amos 5:12-24	*God desires justice, not offerings*
TUESDAY	Zechariah 7:1-14	*Fasting versus justice and mercy*
WEDNESDAY	Luke 19:11-27	*A parable about life in the church*
THURSDAY	Proverbs 15:8-11, 24-33	*God welcomes the righteous*
FRIDAY	Jude 5-21	*Warning against sinners in the church*
SATURDAY	Psalm 50	*Offer to God a sacrifice of thanksgiving*

Sunday between November 6 and 12 inclusive (Proper 27)

SUNDAY	Job 19:23-27a	*I know that my Redeemer lives*
	Psalm 17:1-9	*Keep me as the apple of your eye*
	or Haggai 1:15b—2:9	*The promise to restore Judah*
	Psalm 145:1-5, 17-21	*Great is the LORD*
	or Psalm 98	*Earth sees the victory of God*
	2 Thessalonians 2:1-5, 13-17	*The coming of Christ Jesus*
	Luke 20:27-38	*Jesus speaks of the resurrection*
MONDAY	Deuteronomy 25:5-10	*Instructions for a levirate marriage*
TUESDAY	Genesis 38:1-26	*Tamar and levirate marriages*
WEDNESDAY	Luke 20:1-8	*Jesus' authority questioned*
THURSDAY	Exodus 3:13-20	*God appears to Moses*
FRIDAY	Acts 24:10-23	*Paul testifies to the resurrection*
SATURDAY	Psalm 122	*God will keep you forever*

Sunday between November 13 and 19 inclusive (Proper 28)

SUNDAY	Malachi 4:1-2a	*A day of healing sun for the righteous*
	Psalm 98	*God judges the world*
	or Isaiah 65:17-25	*God promises a new heaven and a new earth*
	Isaiah 12	*In your midst the Holy One of Israel*
	2 Thessalonians 3:6-13	*Do what is right for the sake of Christ*
	Luke 21:5-19	*Jesus speaks of suffering for his sake*
MONDAY	1 Samuel 28:3-19	*Saul warned of God's judgment*
TUESDAY	2 Samuel 21:1-14	*Violence comes on Saul's household*
WEDNESDAY	Luke 17:20-37	*The judgment coming*
THURSDAY	Ezekiel 10:1-19	*God's glory leaves Jerusalem*
FRIDAY	2 Thessalonians 1:3-12	*God's judgment*
SATURDAY	Psalm 141	*God is my refuge*

Christ the King (Proper 29)

SUNDAY	Jeremiah 23:1-6	*Coming of the shepherd and righteous Branch*
	Psalm 46	*The God of Jacob is our stronghold*
	or Jeremiah 23:1-6	*Coming of the shepherd and righteous Branch*
	Luke 1:68-79	*God has raised up for us a mighty savior*
	Colossians 1:11-20	*A hymn to Christ, firstborn of all creation*
	Luke 23:33-43	*Jesus is crucified between two thieves*
MONDAY	Psalm 24	*The King of glory comes*
TUESDAY	Psalm 47	*God reigns*
WEDNESDAY	Luke 18:15-17	*Receiving the kingdom of God*
THURSDAY	Isaiah 33:17-22	*Our God rules*
FRIDAY	Revelation 21:5-27	*God reigns in the holy city*

Last day of the three-year cycle

SATURDAY	John 21:24-25	*"the world itself could not contain the books that would be written"*

Lesser Festivals

Lesser Festivals

St. Andrew, Apostle

NOVEMBER 30   **Ezekiel 3:16-21**   *A sentinel for the house of Israel*
                   Psalm 19:1-6   *The heavens declare God's glory*
                   Romans 10:10-18   *Faith comes from the word of Christ*
                   John 1:35-42   *Jesus calls Andrew*

St. Thomas, Apostle

DECEMBER 21   **Judges 6:36-40**   *God affirms Gideon's calling*
                   Psalm 136:1-4, 23-26   *God's mercy endures forever*
                   Ephesians 4:11-16   *The body of Christ has various gifts*
                   John 14:1-7   *Jesus, the way, the truth, the life*

St. Stephen, Deacon and Martyr

DECEMBER 26   **2 Chronicles 24:17-22**   *Zechariah is stoned to death*
                   Psalm 17:1-9, 15   *I call upon you, O God*
                   Acts 6:8—7:2a, 51-60   *Stephen is stoned to death*
                   Matthew 23:34-39   *Jesus laments that Jerusalem kills her prophets*

St. John, Apostle and Evangelist

DECEMBER 27   **Genesis 1:1-5, 26-31**   *Humankind is created by God*
                   Psalm 116:12-19   *The death of faithful servants*
                   1 John 1:1—2:2   *Jesus, the word of life*
                   John 21:20-25   *The beloved disciple remains with Jesus*

The Holy Innocents, Martyrs

DECEMBER 28   **Jeremiah 31:15-17**   *Rachel weeps for her children*
                   Psalm 124   *We have escaped like a bird*
                   1 Peter 4:12-19   *Continue to do good while suffering*
                   Matthew 2:13-18   *Herod kills innocent children*

The Name of Jesus

JANUARY 1   **Numbers 6:22-27**   *The Aaronic blessing*
                   Psalm 8   *How exalted is your name in all the world*
                   Galatians 4:4-7   *We are no longer slaves, but children*
                   or **Philippians 2:5-11**   *God takes on human form*
                   Luke 2:15-21   *The child is named Jesus*

The Confession of St. Peter

JANUARY 18   Acts 4:8-13   *Salvation is in no one other than Jesus*
Psalm 18:1-7, 16-19   *My God, my rock, worthy of praise*
1 Corinthians 10:1-5   *Drinking from the spiritual rock of Christ*
Matthew 16:13-19   *Peter confesses, You are the Messiah*

The Conversion of St. Paul

JANUARY 25   Acts 9:1-22   *Saul is converted to Christ*
Psalm 67   *Let all the peoples praise you, O God*
Galatians 1:11-24   *Paul receives a revelation of Christ*
Luke 21:10-19   *The end times will require endurance*

The Presentation of Our Lord

FEBRUARY 2   Malachi 3:1-4   *My messenger, a refiner and purifier*
Psalm 84   *How dear to me is your dwelling, O LORD*
or Psalm 24:7-10   *Lift up your heads*
Hebrews 2:14-18   *Jesus shares human flesh and sufferings*
Luke 2:22-40   *The child is brought to the temple*

St. Matthias, Apostle

FEBRUARY 24 Isaiah 66:1-2   *Heaven is God's throne, earth is God's footstool*
Psalm 56   *I am bound by the vow I made to you*
Acts 1:15-26   *The apostles cast lots for Matthias*
Luke 6:12-16   *Jesus calls the Twelve*

The Annunciation of Our Lord

MARCH 25   Isaiah 7:10-14   *A young woman will bear a son*
Psalm 45   *Your name will be remembered*
or Psalm 40:5-10   *I love to do your will, O God*
Hebrews 10:4-10   *The offering of Jesus' body sanctifies us*
Luke 1:26-38   *The angel greets Mary*

St. Mark, Evangelist

APRIL 25   Isaiah 52:7-10   *The messenger announces salvation*
Psalm 57   *Be merciful to me, O God*
2 Timothy 4:6-11, 18   *The good fight of faith*
Mark 1:1-15   *The beginning of the gospel of Jesus Christ*

St. Philip and St. James, Apostles

MAY 1	Isaiah 30:18-21	*God's mercy and justice*
	Psalm 44:1-3, 20-26	*Save us for the sake of your love*
	2 Corinthians 4:1-6	*Proclaiming Jesus Christ as Lord*
	John 14:8-14	*The Son and the Father are one*

The Visitation

MAY 31	1 Samuel 2:1-10	*Hannah's thanksgiving*
	Psalm 113	*God, the helper of the needy*
	Romans 12:9-16b	*Rejoice with those who rejoice*
	Luke 1:39-57	*Mary greets Elizabeth*

St. Barnabas, Apostle

JUNE 11	Isaiah 42:5-12	*The LORD calls us in righteousness*
	Psalm 112	*Happy are the God-fearing*
	Acts 11:19-30; 13:1-3	*Barnabas and Saul are set apart*
	Matthew 10:7-16	*Jesus sends out the Twelve*

The Nativity of St. John the Baptist

JUNE 24	Malachi 3:1-4	*My messenger, a refiner and purifier*
	Psalm 141	*My eyes are turned to God*
	Acts 13:13-26	*The gospel for the descendants of Abraham*
	Luke 1:57-67 [68-80]	*The birth and naming of John*

St. Peter and St. Paul, Apostles

JUNE 29	Ezekiel 34:11-16	*God, the true shepherd*
	Psalm 87:1-2, 5-7	*Glorious things are spoken of you*
	1 Corinthians 3:16-23	*All belongs to Christ*
	Mark 8:27-35	*Peter confesses, You are the Messiah*

St. Mary Magdalene

JULY 22	Ruth 1:6-18	*Ruth stays with Naomi*
	or Exodus 2:1-10	*Moses is saved by Pharaoh's daughter*
	Psalm 73:23-28	*I will speak of all God's works*
	Acts 13:26-33a	*The raising of Jesus fulfills God's promise*
	John 20:1-2, 11-18	*Mary Magdalene meets Jesus in the garden*

St. James the Elder, Apostle

JULY 25	1 Kings 19:9-18	*Elijah hears God in the midst of silence*
	Psalm 7:1-10	*God, my shield and defense*
	Acts 11:27-12:3a	*James is killed by Herod*
	Mark 10:35-45	*Whoever wishes to be great must serve*

Mary, Mother of Our Lord

AUGUST 15	Isaiah 61:7-11	*God will cause righteousness to spring up*
	Psalm 45:11-15	*God's name will be remembered*
	Galatians 4:4-7	*We are no longer slaves, but children*
	Luke 1:46-55	*Mary's thanksgiving*

St. Bartholomew, Apostle

AUGUST 24	Exodus 19:1-6	*Israel is God's priestly kingdom*
	Psalm 12	*A plea for help in evil times*
	1 Corinthians 12:27-31a	*The body of Christ*
	John 1:43-51	*Jesus says: Follow me*

Holy Cross Day

SEPTEMBER 14	Numbers 21:4b-9	*A bronze serpent in the wilderness*
	Psalm 98:1-4	*The LORD has done marvelous things*
	or Psalm 78:1-2, 34-38	*God was their rock*
	1 Corinthians 1:18-24	*The cross is the power of God*
	John 3:13-17	*The Son of Man will be lifted up*

St. Matthew, Apostle and Evangelist

SEPTEMBER 21	Ezekiel 2:8—3:11	*A prophet to the house of Israel*
	Psalm 119:33-40	*Give me understanding*
	Ephesians 2:4-10	*By grace you have been saved*
	Matthew 9:9-13	*Jesus calls to Matthew: Follow me*

St. Michael and All Angels

SEPTEMBER 29	Daniel 10:10-14; 12:1-3	*Michael shall arise*
	Psalm 103:1-5, 20-22	*Bless the LORD, you angels*
	Revelation 12:7-12	*Michael defeats Satan in a cosmic battle*
	Luke 10:17-20	*Jesus gives his followers authority*

St. Luke, Evangelist

OCTOBER 18   **Isaiah 43:8-13**   *You are my witness*
               or **Isaiah 35:5-8**   *God heals the blind and deaf*
               Psalm 124   *Our help is in God*
               2 Timothy 4:5-11   *The good fight of faith*
               Luke 1:1-4; 24:44-53   *Luke witnesses to the ministry of Jesus*

St. Simon and St. Jude, Apostles

OCTOBER 28   **Jeremiah 26:[1-6] 7-16**   *Jeremiah promises the judgment of God*
               Psalm 11   *Take refuge in God*
               1 John 4:1-6   *Do not believe every spirit of this world*
               John 14:21-27   *Those who love Jesus will keep his word*

Reformation Day

OCTOBER 31   **Jeremiah 31:31-34**   *I will write my law in their hearts*
               Psalm 46   *The God of Jacob is our stronghold*
               Romans 3:19-28   *Justified by God's grace as a gift*
               John 8:31-36   *The truth will set you free*

All Saints Day

NOVEMBER 1 | A   **Revelation 7:9-17**   *The multitudes of heaven worship the Lamb*
                   Psalm 34:1-10, 22   *Fear the LORD, you saints*
                   1 John 3:1-3   *We are God's children*
                   Matthew 5:1-12   *Blessed are the poor in spirit*

               B   **Isaiah 25:6-9**   *A feast of rich foods*
                   or **Wisdom of Solomon 3:1-9**   *The righteous are with God*
                   Psalm 24   *They shall receive a blessing from God*
                   Revelation 21:1-6a   *A new heaven and a new earth*
                   John 11:32-44   *The raising of Lazarus*

               C   **Daniel 7:1-3, 15-18**   *The holy ones of the Most High*
                   Psalm 149   *Sing praise for God's goodness*
                   Ephesians 1:11-23   *God made Christ head over all*
                   Luke 6:20-31   *Jesus speaks blessings and woes*

New Year's Eve

DECEMBER 31   **Ecclesiastes 3:1-13**   *For everything there is a season*
               Psalm 8   *How exalted is your name*
               Revelation 21:1-6a   *A new heaven and a new earth*
               Matthew 25:31-46   *The sheep and the goats*

Day of Thanksgiving

A	Deuteronomy 8:7-18	*A land of streams*
	Psalm 65	*You crown the year with your goodness*
	2 Corinthians 9:6-15	*God provides every blessing in abundance*
	Luke 17:11-19	*The healed leper gives thanks to Jesus*
B	Joel 2:21-27	*The promise to restore Jerusalem*
	Psalm 126	*Sowing in tears, reaping with joy*
	1 Timothy 2:1-7	*Make thanksgivings*
	Matthew 6:25-33	*God will care for all our needs*
C	Deuteronomy 26:1-11	*The offering of the first fruits*
	Psalm 100	*Enter the gates of the LORD with thanksgiving*
	Philippians 4:4-9	*Do not worry about anything*
	John 6:25-35	*Jesus, the bread of life*

Alternate Daily Readings

When a lesser festival occurs on a Sunday, these readings may be used during the following week

MONDAY	Deuteronomy 7:1-11	*God calls a holy people*
TUESDAY	Numbers 11:16-30	*God's spirit comes on the elders*
WEDNESDAY	John 15:1-17	*Abiding in the vine*
THURSDAY	Isaiah 62:1-12	*God marries the people*
FRIDAY	Colossians 1:3-23a	*The saints bearing fruit*
SATURDAY	Psalm 99	*God praised by the faithful people*

Index
to Daily Readings

The readings in this index are appointed for Monday through Saturday. The index for Sunday and festival readings begins on page 112.

Daily reading	Year	Day	Week	*RCL Occurrence
Genesis				
1:1—2:4a	A	Dec 29		A(B)V
1:1—2:4a	B	Dec 29		A(B)V
1:1—2:4a	B	M	Easter	A(B)V
1:1—2:4a	C	Dec 29		A(B)V
3:14-24	B	Th	Pr. 6	(B)
4:1-16	A	Th	1 Lent	—
6:11-22	C	M	1 Advent	—
7:11—8:5	A	M	Pr. 14	(V)
8:1-19; 9:8-13	A	T	1 Advent	(V)
11:1-9	B	Th	Pentecost	altC
12:1-9	B	M	3 Epiphany	(A)
14:17-24	B	Th	Pr. 24	—
15:1-18	A	Th	2 Advent	(C)
16:1-14	B	Th	2 Epiphany	—
17:1-14, 23-27	B	M	Baptism of Our Lord	(B)
17:15-22	A	M	4 Advent	(B)
18:1-14	A	M	3 Easter	(C)
18:1-14	B	M	Pr. 12	(C)
19:15-29	A	T	Pr. 14	—
21:1-7	B	M	2 Lent	—
21:1-21	A	T	4 Advent	—
22:1-14	C	M	Pr. 5	V
22:1-19	B	T	2 Lent	V
24:1-27	A	M	3 Lent	—
25:19-28	C	M	4 Advent	—
27:1-29	A	M	Pr. 20	—
28:10-17	A	T	Pr. 20	—
29:1-14	A	T	3 Lent	—
30:1-24	C	T	4 Advent	—
31:1-7, 17-26, 44-50	A	Th	7 Epiphany	—

Daily reading		Year	Day	Week	RCL Occurrence
(Gen.)	33:1-17	C	M	7 Epiphany	—
	34:1-31	C	M	Passion	—
	35:1-15	A	M	Baptism of Our Lord	—
	37:2-11	A	Th	4 Advent	—
	37:12-36	A	M	Pr. 19	—
	38:1-26	C	T	Pr. 27	—
	39:1-23	C	M	Pr. 18	—
	41:14-36	C	M	Pr. 10	—
	41:37-49	C	T	Pr. 10	—
	41:53—42:17	A	T	Pr. 19	—
	43:1-15	B	M	Pr. 15	—
	45:1-15	B	T	Pr. 15	(C)
	45:1-20	A	Th	Pr. 19	(C)
	45:25—46:7	B	T	3 Epiphany	—
	47:13-26	B	Th	Pr. 15	—
	48:8-19	B	M	4 Easter	—
	49:1-2, 8-13, 21-26	A	Th	4 Epiphany	—
Exodus					
	1:15—2:10	A	Th	1 Christmas	—
	1:22—2:10	B	Jan 7		—
	2:11-25	B	Jan 8		—
	3:13-20	C	Th	Pr. 27	—
	4:1-17	B	M	Pr. 25	—
	5:10-23	C	Th	Ash Wednesday	—
	6:1-13	C	F	Ash Wednesday	—
	7:14-24	B	M	Pr. 7	—
	9:13-35	B	T	Pr. 7	—
	12:1-13, 21-28	A	M	2 Epiphany	(ABC)
	13:11-16	B	T	1 Christmas	—
	13:17-22	A	M	5 Easter	—
	14:10-31; 15:20-21	A	M	Easter	V
	15:1-18	A	Sa	Easter	(V)
	15:22-27	B	M	4 Lent	—
	16:2-15, 31-35	A	Th	Pr. 13	(B)
	16:13-26	B	T	Pr. 4	(B)
	18:1-12	C	M	Pr. 11	—
	18:13-27	B	M	Pr. 21	—
	19:7-20	A	M	Pr. 23	(A)
	19:7-25	B	M	Transfiguration	(A)
	20:1-21	A	M	6 Epiphany	(B)
	23:1-9	C	Th	Pr. 20	—
	24:1-11	A	T	3 Easter	—
	24:1-11	B	T	Pr. 12	—
	25:1-22	B	T	Holy Trinity	—
	28:29-38	B	M	7 Easter	—

Daily reading		Year	Day	Week	RCL Occurrence
(Exod.)	30:22-38	B	T	Baptism of Our Lord	—
	31:12-18	B	M	Pr. 4	—
	32:1-14	B	M	Pr. 17	(C)
	32:15-35	B	T	Pr. 17	—
	33:1-6	C	M	2 Lent	—
	33:7-23	A	M	Transfiguration	—
	34:1-9, 27-28	A	M	1 Lent	—
	40:1-15	C	M	5 Lent	—
	40:16-38	C	M	7 Easter	—
Leviticus					
	4:27-31; 5:14-16	A	M	Pr. 18	—
	5:1-13	C	Th	7 Epiphany	—
	9:1-4, 22-24	A	M	7 Easter	—
	9:22—10:11	C	M	Pr. 8	—
	12:1-8	B	M	1 Christmas	—
	13:1-17	B	M	6 Epiphany	—
	14:1-20	B	T	6 Epiphany	—
	14:33-53	C	T	Pr. 23	—
	15:19-31	B	T	Pr. 8	—
	15:25-31; 22:1-9	A	Th	Pr. 5	—
	16:1-5, 20-28	A	Th	Pr. 18	—
	19:1-4, 32-37	C	Th	Pr. 10	(A)
	19:9-18	C	Th	5 Easter	(A)
	21:1-15	B	M	Pr. 8	—
	23:26-41	C	M	4 Lent	—
	24:10-23	A	M	7 Epiphany	—
	25:1-19	C	T	4 Lent	—
	26:3-20	A	M	Pr. 10	—
Numbers					
	3:5-13	C	Th	2 Advent	—
	6:22-27	B	Th	Holy Trinity	Jan 1
	8:5-22	B	T	7 Easter	—
	9:15-23	B	M	Holy Trinity	—
	11:16-23, 31-32	B	M	Pr. 13	—
	11:24-30	A	Th	Pentecost	altA
	12:1-15	C	M	Pr. 23	—
	13:17-27	C	Th	3 Lent	—
	14:10b-24	C	T	2 Lent	—
	16:1-9	C	M	3 Advent	—
	16:20-35	C	T	3 Advent	—
	16:41-50	A	Th	7 Easter	—
	17:1-11	C	M	1 Advent	—
	20:1-13	B	T	4 Lent	—
	21:4-9	A	Th	2 Lent	B

Daily reading		Year	Day	Week	RCL Occurrence
(Num.)	22:1-21	B	M	4 Epiphany	—
	22:22-38	B	T	4 Epiphany	—
	24:1-14	C	Th	Pentecost	—
	24:15-19	C	Jan 10		—
	27:1-11	C	Th	Baptism of Our Lord	—
	27:12-23	C	M	5 Epiphany	—
Deuteronomy					
	1:1-18	B	T	Pr. 21	—
	4:21-40	B	Th	Pr. 17	—
	5:1-21	B	M	Pr. 23	(B)
	5:22-33	A	M	6 Easter	—
	5:22-33	B	T	Pr. 23	—
	6:1-9, 20-25	A	M	Pr. 25	(B)
	6:10-25	B	M	Pr. 26	—
	7:1-11	B	M	6 Easter	—
	7:12-26	C	Th	Pr. 18	—
	8:1-10	A	M	Pr. 13	—
	8:1-20	B	T	Pr. 13	—
	10:10-22	A	T	Pr. 25	—
	11:1-17	B	T	6 Easter	—
	12:1-12	C	Th	Pr. 11	—
	17:2-13	A	T	Pr. 18	—
	17:14-20	A	Th	Pr. 24	—
	22:13-30	B	M	Pr. 22	—
	23:21—24:4, 10-18	A	T	6 Epiphany	—
	24:1-5	B	T	Pr. 22	—
	24:17-22	B	Th	Pr. 27	—
	25:5-10	C	M	Pr. 27	—
	26:1-15	A	T	Pr. 13	(C)
	28:1-24	A	T	Pr. 10	—
	28:58—29:1	B	T	Pr. 26	—
	31:1-13	A	T	6 Easter	—
	32:1-14	A	M	8 Epiphany	—
	32:15-27, 39-43	C	Th	Pr. 8	—
	32:18-20, 28-39	A	T	Pr. 16	—
Joshua					
	1:1-11	A	M	Pr. 6	—
	3:1-17	A	T	Easter	—
	4:1-10, 19-24	A	Th	Pr. 21	—
	6:1-21	B	Th	Pr. 18	—
	7:1, 10-26	C	Th	Pr. 15	—
	8:1-22	B	T	Pr. 18	—
	8:30-35	A	M	Pr. 4	—
	10:1-14	B	Th	Pr. 7	—

Daily reading		Year	Day	Week	RCL Occurrence
(Josh.)	10:16-27	C	M	Easter	—
	23:1-16	C	Th	Pr. 9	—
	24:1-2a, 14-28	A	T	Pr. 4	(B)
Judges					
	4:1-10, 12-16	C	M	Baptism of Our Lord	—
	4:17-23; 5:24-31a	C	Th	Easter	—
	5:12-21	C	T	Baptism of Our Lord	—
	6:11-24	A	M	3 Epiphany	—
	6:36-40	A	Th	2 Easter	—
	7:12-22	A	T	3 Epiphany	—
	9:7-15	C	T	5 Lent	—
	11:29-40	C	T	Pr. 5	—
	13:2-24	B	Th	4 Advent	—
	15:9-20	B	Th	Pr. 18	—
	16:1-22	A	M	Pr. 21	—
	16:23-31	A	T	Pr. 21	—
	19:22-30	C	T	Passion	—
Ruth					
	1:1-18	A	M	4 Epiphany	—
	1:1-22	B	M	Pr. 27	—
	2:1-16	A	T	4 Epiphany	—
	2:1-23	B	T	Pr. 14	—
	3:1-13; 4:13-22	A	Th	4 Epiphany	—
	4:7-22	B	T	Pr. 27	—
1 Samuel					
	1:1-18	B	M	4 Advent	—
	1:19-28	B	T	4 Advent	—
	2:1-10	B	Sa	4 Advent	—
	2:1-10	C	Th	Pr. 25	—
	2:27-36	A	T	Pr. 26	—
	3:1-19	A	T	Pr. 6	B
	4:1b-11	C	Sa	Holy Saturday	—
	5:1-12	C	M	Pr. 15	—
	6:1-16	C	T	Pr. 15	—
	7:3-13	A	M	Pr. 16	—
	7:18-29	C	T	1 Advent	—
	8:1-18	B	M	Pr. 24	—
	9:15—10:1b	C	M	5 Epiphany	—
	9:27—10:8	B	M	2 Epiphany	—
	10:17-25	B	T	Pr. 24	—
	15:10-31	B	T	2 Epiphany	—
	16:14-23	B	M	Pr. 5	—
	17:1-23	C	M	2 Easter	—

Daily reading	Year	Day	Week	RCL Occurrence
(1 Sam.) 17:32-51	C	T	2 Easter	—
20:1-23, 35-42	C	M	5 Easter	—
21:1-6	B	Th	Pr. 4	—
24:1-22	C	T	7 Epiphany	—
25:1-22	C	M	Pr. 24	—
25:23-35 [36-42]	C	T	Pr. 24	—
28:3-19	C	M	Pr. 28	—
2 Samuel				
1:4-27	C	T	5 Easter	—
5:1-12	B	Th	Pr. 11	—
6:1-15	C	T	Easter	—
7:18-29	C	T	1 Advent	—
11:2-26	A	M	Pr. 17	—
11:27b—12:15a	T	B	Pr. 17	(C)
13:1-22	C	W	Passion	—
18:28—19:8	C	Th	Pr. 6	—
21:1-14	C	T	Pr. 28	—
1 Kings				
3:16-28	A	M	Pr. 12	—
4:29-34	A	T	Pr. 12	—
6:1-22	B	M	3 Lent	—
8:10-13, 22-30	A	Th	Holy Trinity	(C)
8:54-65	A	T	7 Easter	—
10:1-13	A	Jan 7		—
10:14-25	A	Jan 8		—
13:1-10	B	M	Pr. 19	—
13:11-25	B	T	Pr. 19	—
17:1-16	A	T	8 Epiphany	(B)
17:1-16	B	M	Pr. 14	(B)
17:8-16	C	M	4 Epiphany	B
17:17-24	A	M	5 Lent	(C)
18:1-18	B	M	3 Advent	—
18:17-40	B	M	Pr. 5	—
19:1-8	A	Th	1 Lent	(B)
19:1-3, 9-18	A	T	Transfiguration	A
21:1-16	A	M	Pr. 8	—
21:17-29	A	T	Pr. 8	—
2 Kings				
1:1-16	C	T	Pr. 8	—
2:9-22	B	T	3 Advent	(B)
4:1-7	C	Th	4 Lent	—
4:8-17, 32-37	B	M	5 Epiphany	—
4:18-37	A	T	5 Lent	—

Daily reading	Year	Day	Week	RCL Occurrence
(2 Kings) 5:1-13	B	M	Pr. 20	B(C)
5:1-14	A	M	Pr. 15	B(C)
5:1-14	C	T	4 Epiphany	B(C)
6:8-25	B	T	Pr. 25	—
8:1-6	B	T	5 Epiphany	—
11:21—12:16	B	T	Pr. 20	—
17:24-41	C	T	Pr. 18	—
18:1-8, 28-36	C	M	Pr. 22	—
19:8-20, 35-37	C	T	Pr. 22	—
20:1-11	B	Th	Pr. 8	—
22:3-20	A	M	5 Epiphany	—
23:1-8, 21-25	A	T	5 Epiphany	—
24:20—25:14	C	M	6 Epiphany	—
1 Chronicles				
11:1-9	B	T	4 Easter	—
12:16-22	C	M	6 Easter	—
21:1-17	C	M	1 Lent	—
28:1-10	C	M	1 Christmas	—
2 Chronicles				
5:2-14	C	T	7 Easter	—
7:1-11	C	T	1 Christmas	—
12:1-12	C	Th	Pr. 17	—
15:1-15	C	T	6 Easter	—
20:1-22	C	Th	2 Lent	—
30:1-12	C	M	Pr. 6	—
30:13-27	C	T	Pr. 6	—
33:1-17	C	M	Pr. 14	—
34:22-33	C	T	Pr. 14	—
Ezra				
1:1-11	C	T	6 Epiphany	—
6:1-18	B	T	3 Lent	—
9:5-15	B	Th	7 Easter	—
Nehemiah				
1:1-11	C	T	Pr. 4	—
9:1-15	B	M	Pr. 16	—
9:16-31	B	T	Pr. 16	—
13:1-3, 23-31	C	Th	Pr. 23	—
13:15-22	C	M	Pr. 16	—
Esther				
2:1-18	A	M	Christ the King	—
3:7-15	C	M	Pr. 12	—
7:1-10	C	T	Pr. 12	—

Daily reading	Year	Day	Week	RCL Occurrence
(Esther) 8:3-17	A	T	Christ the King	—
9:1-5, 18-23	C	Th	2 Easter	—
Job				
1:1-22	C	Th	1 Lent	—
4:1-21	B	M	1 Lent	—
5:8-27	B	T	1 Lent	—
6:1-13	B	T	5 Epiphany	—
14:1-14	A	Sa	Holy Saturday	—
16:1-21	A	Th	Pr. 28	—
18:1-21	C	M	Pr. 7	—
19:1-22	C	T	Pr. 7	—
19:23-27	B	T	Transfiguration	—
22:21—23:17	C	Th	Pr. 12	—
28:12-28	A	Th	Pr. 4	—
30:16-31	B	Th	6 Epiphany	—
36:24-33; 37:14-24	A	Th	Pr. 14	—
38:1-21	A	M	Holy Trinity	(B)
38:34—39:4, 26—40:5	A	T	Holy Trinity	—
40:6-14; 42:1-6	C	Th	Pr. 19	—
Psalms				
1	C	Sa	8 Epiphany	ABC
3	C	Sa	Pr. 22	—
5	A	Sa	Pr. 26	—
5	B	Sa	Pr. 21	—
5	C	Sa	Pr. 4	—
6	A	Sa	Pr. 7	—
6	B	Sa	6 Epiphany	—
7	A	Sa	Christ the King	—
9:1-14	A	Sa	Pr. 28	—
10	B	M	Passion	—
11	C	Sa	1 Christmas	—
12	C	Sa	Pr. 20	—
13	B	Sa	Pr. 28	—
17	A	Sa	Pr. 17	(C)
17	C	Sa	Pr. 27	(C)
18:1-19	A	Sa	Pr. 14	—
18:1-3, 20-32	A	Sa	Pr. 16	—
20	B	Sa	Holy Trinity	—
20	C	Sa	5 Lent	—
21	A	Sa	2 Advent	—
23	A	Sa	4 Easter	ABC
24	C	M	Christ the King	B
25	C	Sa	Pr. 10	(ABC)
26	B	Sa	Pr. 23	(A)

Daily reading		Year	Day	Week	RCL Occurrence
(Ps.)	27	B	Sa	2 Advent	(A)C
	27:7-14	A	Sa	3 Epiphany	(A)
	28	A	Sa	Pr. 21	—
	29	A	Sa	Holy Trinity	ABC
	29	C	Sa	7 Easter	ABC
	32	B	Sa	Ash Wednesday	AC
	32	C	Sa	Pr. 15	AC
	34	A	Sa	Pr. 23	AB
	35:1-10	B	Sa	4 Epiphany	—
	36	B	Sa	Pr. 15	(C)
	37:1-17	A	Sa	4 Epiphany	(C)
	37:23-40	B	Sa	Pr. 24	(C)
	38	A	Sa	1 Lent	—
	38	B	Sa	7 Epiphany	—
	38	C	Sa	7 Epiphany	—
	39	C	Sa	3 Lent	—
	40:1-8	A	Sa	Pr. 5	A
	40:6-17	A	Sa	2 Epiphany	(A)
	42	A	Sa	3 Advent	C(V)
	44	B	T	Passion	—
	45:6-17	B	Sa	8 Epiphany	—
	46	B	Sa	3 Epiphany	CV
	47	C	T	Christ the King	ABC
	48	C	Sa	Pentecost	—
	50	C	Sa	Pr. 26	(AB)
	51	B	Sa	Pr. 26	ABC
	52	A	Sa	Pr. 4	—
	52	B	Sa	Pr. 6	—
	53	C	Sa	4 Lent	—
	55:16-23	C	Sa	Pr. 12	—
	56	C	Sa	4 Epiphany	—
	57	C	Sa	Pr. 24	—
	61	C	Sa	Pr. 23	—
	62	C	Sa	Pr. 21	(B)
	63	A	Sa	Pr. 27	(C)
	64	C	Sa	Pr. 7	—
	65	B	Sa	Pr. 7	AC
	68:1-19, 19-20	C	Sa	Pr. 5	A
	69:1-5, 30-36	B	Sa	Baptism of Our Lord	(A)
	71:1-16	A	Sa	2 Christmas	(C)
	72:1-19	A	Jan 12		(ABC)
	73	C	Sa	Pr. 19	—
	74	B	Sa	Pr. 5	—
	75	A	Sa	Pr. 11	—
	76	B	Sa	Christ the King	—
	77	B	Sa	1 Lent	—

Daily reading		Year	Day	Week	RCL Occurrence
(Ps.)	78:1-8, 17-29	A	Sa	Pr. 13	(B)
	78:1-4, 52-72	B	Sa	Pr. 4	—
	79	B	Sa	1 Advent	—
	80	B	Sa	5 Easter	(ABC)
	81	A	Sa	3 Lent	(B)
	81	B	Sa	Pr. 14	(B)
	84	C	Sa	Pr. 25	(C)
	85	C	Sa	3 Advent	(AB)
	86	B	Sa	2 Epiphany	(A)
	87	A	Sa	Pr. 15	—
	88	B	Sa	Pr. 8	—
	89:1-18	C	Sa	Pr. 14	(AB)
	89:5-37	A	Sa	Baptism of Our Lord	(AB)
	90	C	Sa	1 Advent	(AB)
	92	A	Sa	Pr. 10	(BC)
	93	A	Sa	6 Easter	B
	94	B	Sa	Pr. 27	—
	95	B	Sa	4 Easter	A
	96	A	Dec 28		(AC) altABC
	97	A	Dec 30		C altABC
	98	A	Sa	Pr. 24	ABC
	99	A	Sa	7 Easter	AC
	100	B	Dec 28		A
	100	B	Sa	Pr. 11	A
	100	C	Sa	4 Easter	A
	101	C	Sa	Pr. 18	—
	102:1-17	A	Sa	5 Easter	—
	102:12-28	B	Sa	5 Epiphany	—
	104:1-9, 24-35	A	Sa	Pentecost	ABC
	104:1-24	B	T	Easter	(ABC)
	104:10-28	A	Sa	8 Epiphany	(ABC)
	105:1-11, 37-45	A	Sa	Pr. 6	—
	105:1-11, 37-45	B	Sa	2 Lent	—
	105:1-11 [12-41] 42-45	C	Sa	2 Lent	—
	106:1-6, 13-23, 47-48	B	Sa	Pr. 17	—
	106:1-12	A	Sa	Pr. 20	—
	106:1-12	C	Sa	Baptism of Our Lord	—
	107:1-16	B	Sa	4 Lent	(B)
	107:1-3, 33-43	B	Sa	Pr. 13	(B)
	108	C	Sa	Easter	—
	109:21-31	C	Sa	Pr. 16	—
	110	B	Jan 12		C
	111	B	Sa	Pr. 12	BC
	112	B	Sa	Pr. 22	C
	113	C	Sa	4 Advent	C
	114	A	Sa	2 Easter	V

Daily reading		Year	Day	Week	RCL Occurrence
(Ps.)	115	C	Sa	7 Easter	—
	115	C	Sa	5 Epiphany	—
	119:9-16	A	Sa	6 Epiphany	altB
	119:9-16	B	Sa	5 Lent	altB
	119:17-24	B	Sa	Pr. 25	—
	119:41-48	A	Sa	Pr. 25	—
	119:57-64	A	Sa	7 Epiphany	—
	119:65-72	A	Sa	Pr. 18	—
	119:65-72	C	Sa	Pr. 17	—
	119:73-80	C	Sa	Pr. 9	—
	119:81-88	B	Sa	Pr. 9	—
	119:89-96	C	Sa	3 Epiphany	—
	119:97-104	B	Sa	Pr. 16	—
	119:97-104	C	Sa	Pr. 11	—
	119:105-112	A	Sa	5 Epiphany	—
	119:121-128	A	Sa	Pr. 12	—
	119:161-168	A	Sa	Pr. 8	—
	119:169-176	B	Sa	Pr. 19	—
	120	C	Sa	6 Epiphany	—
	121	C	Sa	3 Easter	A
	122	C	Sa	2 Easter	A
	122	C	Sa	Pr. 27	A
	124	A	Sa	1 Advent	—
	124	C	Sa	Holy Trinity	—
	125	B	Sa	3 Advent	—
	125	C	Sa	6 Easter	—
	126	C	Sa	2 Advent	B
	127	C	Sa	Pr. 13	—
	128	A	Sa	2 Lent	—
	130	C	Sa	Pr. 6	AB
	131	A	Sa	Pr. 9	A
	132	B	Sa	6 Easter	(B)
	133	A	Sa	Pr. 19	B
	133	C	Sa	5 Easter	B
	134	A	Sa	3 Easter	—
	135	B	Sa	2 Easter	—
	136	B	Dec 30		(V)
	136	B	Sa	Easter	(V)
	137	B	W	Passion	—
	139:1-18	B	Sa	Pr. 20	(B)
	140	C	Sa	Pr. 8	—
	141	C	Sa	Pr. 28	—
	142	B	Sa	Pr. 10	—
	143	A	Sa	5 Lent	V
	144	A	Sa	Pr. 22	—
	144	C	Sa	2 Easter	—

Daily reading		Year	Day	Week	RCL Occurrence
(Ps.)	145	B	Sa	1 Christmas	(AB)
	145	C	Sa	2 Epiphany	(AB)
	146	A	Sa	4 Lent	(A)BC
	148	C	Dec 28		—
	149	B	Sa	Pentecost	—
	150	B	Sa	3 Easter	—
	150	C	Dec 30		—
Proverbs					
	1:1-7, 20-33	A	Th	Pr. 12	—
	2:1-15	A	Th	6 Epiphany	—
	3:5-18	A	T	5 Easter	—
	3:13-26	C	M	Holy Trinity	—
	4:1-9	C	T	Holy Trinity	—
	4:10-27	A	T	Pr. 6	—
	5:1-23	C	T	8 Epiphany	—
	6:6-23	A	T	5 Epiphany	—
	8:1-21	B	T	3 Epiphany	(CV)
	8:32—9:6	A	Th	3 Easter	(BV)
	9:1-18	C	T	Pr. 11	(B)
	11:23-30	A	T	Pr. 10	—
	14:12-31	C	M	Pr. 20	—
	15:8-11, 24-33	C	Th	Pr. 26	—
	16:1-20	A	Th	Pr. 25	—
	17:1-5	C	T	Pr. 20	—
	22:2-16	C	M	Pr. 21	—
	25:11-22	A	Th	7 Epiphany	—
	28:3-10	C	T	Pr. 21	—
	30:1-9	B	Th	1 Lent	—
Ecclesiastes					
	2:1-17	C	M	Pr. 13	—
	3:1-8	C	Sa	Ash Wednesday	Jan 1
	3:16—4:8	C	T	Pr. 13	—
	12:1-8, 13-14	C	Th	Pr. 13	—
Song of Solomon					
	2:3-15	A	Th	Easter	—
	3:1-11	B	Th	Easter	—
	4:9—5:1	C	Th	2 Epiphany	—
	7:10—8:4	A	Th	Pr. 23	—
	8:5-14	A	Th	Pr. 22	—
Isaiah					
	1:24-31	C	Th	1 Advent	—
	2:5-17	C	M	Pr. 17	—

Daily reading		Year	Day	Week	RCL Occurrence
(Isa.)	4:2-6	B	T	2 Advent	—
	5:1-7	B	M	5 Easter	A
	7:1-9	C	Th	Pr. 22	(A)
	8:1-15	C	Th	5 Epiphany	—
	9:2b-7	A	Dec 27		(A) alt ABC
	10:12-20	B	Th	Pr. 19	—
	19:18-24	C	T	2 Advent	—
	24:1-16a	A	M	2 Advent	—
	25:6-10	B	Th	Pr. 12	(A)
	26:1-15	B	Th	2 Easter	—
	26:7-15	B	M	2 Advent	—
	26:16—27:1	B	Th	Pr. 5	—
	27:1-6	A	T	Pr. 22	—
	28:14-22	A	Th	Pr. 16	—
	29:17-24	A	M	3 Advent	—
	30:18-26	B	M	7 Epiphany	—
	32:9-20	B	T	5 Easter	—
	33:10-16	B	Th	Pr. 16	—
	33:17-22	C	Th	Christ the King	—
	38:10-20	B	Sa	Pr. 18	—
	40:1-11	A	T	2 Advent	B
	40:1-11	C	M	2 Advent	B
	41:1-13	A	Th	Pr. 20	—
	41:14-20	B	Th	Baptism of Our Lord	—
	42:14-21	A	T	4 Lent	(A)
	42:14-21	C	Th	4 Advent	(A)
	43:8-13	B	M	5 Lent	A
	44:1-8	B	T	5 Lent	(A)
	45:8-17	B	Jan 10		—
	48:12-21	A	Th	2 Epiphany	—
	49:5-12	B	Th	1 Christmas	A
	51:7-16	A	Th	Baptism of Our Lord	—
	53:1-12	A	T	2 Epiphany	ABC
	54:1-8	C	M	2 Epiphany	—
	54:4-10	A	Th	1 Advent	—
	54:11-17	C	Th	Pr. 24	—
	55:1-9	B	Th	Pr. 13	(A)CV
	56:1-8	C	Th	Pr. 4	(A)
	57:24-21	C	T	Pr. 17	—
	58:1-12	A	Sa	Ash Wednesday	(AC)
	59:9-19	A	M	4 Lent	—
	60:17-22	A	Th	4 Lent	—
	61:1-7	C	Th	3 Epiphany	(B)
	62:1-5	B	Th	8 Epiphany	C
	62:6-12	B	Dec 27		ABC
	65:17-25	A	M	2 Lent	altC

Daily reading		Year	Day	Week	RCL Occurrence
(Isa.)	65:17-25	B	Th	5 Easter	altC
	66:7-13	A	Th	8 Epiphany	(C)
	66:18-23	A	T	Pr. 15	—
Jeremiah					
	1:4-10	A	T	Baptism of Our Lord	C
	1:4-10	B	Th	Pr. 20	C
	1:11-19	C	Th	4 Epiphany	—
	2:4-13	A	Th	3 Lent	—
	3:6-14	B	Th	Pr. 22	—
	3:19-25	C	T	2 Epiphany	—
	6:10-19	C	M	Pr. 9	—
	8:4-13	C	T	Pr. 9	—
	8:14-22	C	Th	Pr. 5	—
	11:1-17	C	M	3 Lent	—
	13:1-11	A	Th	Pr. 9	—
	16:1-13	B	M	Pr. 9	—
	16:14-21	B	T	Pr. 9	—
	17:5-18	A	Th	Pr. 17	(C)
	18:1-11	A	Th	Pr. 8	—
	22:1-9	B	T	Pr. 6	—
	22:11-17	C	T	6 Epiphany	—
	23:1-8	A	Th	4 Easter	(BC)
	24:1-10	C	M	8 Epiphany	—
	26:1-12	A	M	Pr. 7	—
	27:1-11, 16-22	A	M	Pr. 9	—
	28:10-17	A	T	Pr. 9	(A)
	29:1-14	B	Th	4 Epiphany	—
	29:10-19	C	T	8 Epiphany	—
	30:1-11a	B	M	3 Easter	—
	30:12-22	B	Th	2 Lent	—
	31:1-6	B	Th	Pr. 14	altA
	31:15-22	A	T	1 Christmas	—
	32:1-9, 36-41	A	Th	5 Lent	—
	33:1-11	B	Th	Pr. 25	—
	33:14-26	C	Th	Pr. 14	(C)
	36:1-4, 20-26	C	M	3 Epiphany	—
	36:27-32	C	T	3 Epiphany	—
	38:1-13	A	T	Pr. 7	—
	50:1-7	B	M	Pr. 11	—
	50:17-20	C	M	4 Easter	—
Lamentations					
	3:1-9, 19-24	B	Sa	Holy Saturday	—

Daily reading	Year	Day	Week	RCL Occurrence
Ezekiel				
1:1—2:1	C	M	Transfiguration	—
2:8—3:11	B	Th	Pr. 9	—
3:12-21	C	Th	7 Easter	—
10:1-19	C	Th	Pr. 28	—
11:14-25	C	T	Pentecost	—
13:1-16	A	T	Pr. 26	—
16:1-14	B	M	8 Epiphany	—
16:53-63	B	T	8 Epiphany	—
17:1-10	C	T	3 Lent	—
18:5-24	C	Th	Pr. 21	—
19:10-14	A	M	Pr. 22	—
20:1-17	C	T	Pr. 16	—
28:20-26	B	Th	Christ the King	—
31:1-12	B	M	Pr. 6	—
32:1-10	C	Th	Pr. 7	—
33:7-20	A	Th	Christ the King	(A)
34:1-16	A	M	4 Easter	(A)
34:23-31	A	T	4 Easter	(A)
36:22-32	A	T	2 Lent	(V)
37:1-14	B	T	Pentecost	AV altB
37:15-28	C	T	4 Easter	—
39:7-8, 21-29	A	T	Pentecost	—
43:1-12	C	Th	1 Christmas	—
45:1-9	C	T	4 Easter	—
47:1-12	A	T	3 Advent	—
Daniel				
1:1-21	C	Th	Holy Trinity	—
2:1-19	C	Jan 7		—
2:20-23	C	Jan 12		—
2:24-49	C	Jan 8		—
3:1-30	A	M	Pr. 24	—
3:1-30	B	M	2 Easter	—
4:4-18	B	M	Pr. 28	—
4:19-27, 34-37	B	T	Pr. 28	—
5:1-12	C	M	Pr. 25	—
5:13-31	C	T	Pr. 25	—
6:1-28	A	T	Pr. 24	—
6:1-28	B	T	2 Easter	—
7:1-8, 15-18	B	M	Christ the King	—
7:19-27	B	T	Christ the King	—
9:1-14	B	Th	Ash Wednesday	—
9:15-25a	B	F	Ash Wednesday	—
10:2-19	B	T	3 Easter	—
12:1-13	A	Th	Pr. 11	(B)

Daily reading	Year	Day	Week	RCL Occurrence
Hosea				
5:15—6:6	B	Th	3 Easter	A
8:11-14; 10:1-2	A	M	Pr. 5	—
11:1-11	A	M	1 Christmas	—
14:1-9	A	T	Pr. 5	—
Joel				
1:1-14	A	M	Pr. 27	—
2:18-29	A	M	Pentecost	—
2:18-29	B	M	Pentecost	—
2:18-29	C	M	Pentecost	—
3:9-2	A	T	Pr. 27	—
Amos				
2:6-16	B	M	Pr. 10	—
3:13—4:5	B	Th	Pr. 23	—
4:6-13	B	T	Pr. 10	—
5:12-24	C	M	Pr. 26	(B) (altA)
7:1-6	C	M	Pr. 19	—
8:7-14	A	Th	Pr. 27	(C)
9:5-15	A	T	Pr. 23	—
Jonah				
1:1-17	A	M	2 Easter	—
2:1-10	A	T	2 Easter	—
3:1-10	A	Th	Ash Wednesday	(B)
3:1-10	C	T	Pr. 19	(B)
4:1-11	A	F	Ash Wednesday	A
4:1-11	C	Th	Pr. 4	A
Micah				
2:1-13	B	Th	1 Advent	—
4:1-7	B	T	7 Epiphany	—
4:8-13	C	Th	3 Advent	—
5:2-9	A	Jan 10		(C)
6:1-8	B	Th	Pr. 26	A
7:1-7	A	Th	Pr. 7	—
7:8-20	B	Th	4 Easter	—
Nahum				
1:1-13	A	M	Pr. 11	—
Habbakuk				
3:2-15	C	Th	5 Lent	—
Zepheniah				
3:1-13	A	T	Pr. 11	—

Daily reading	Year	Day	Week	RCL Occurrence
Haggai				
2:1-9; 3:20-23	B	Th	5 Lent	—
Zechariah				
1:7-17	A	M	Pr. 28	—
2:1-5; 5:1-4	A	T	Pr. 28	—
3:1-10	C	T	1 Lent	—
7:1-14	C	T	Pr. 26	—
8:1-17	A	Th	3 Advent	—
9:14—10:2	B	T	Pr. 11	—
10:1-12	B	Th	Pr. 21	—
12:1—13:1	B	Th	Pr. 28	—
13:1-9	B	M	1 Advent	—
14:1-9	B	T	1 Advent	—
Malachi				
1:6—2:9	A	Th	Pr. 26	—
2:10—3:1	B	Th	2 Advent	(altC)
3:13—4:6	B	Th	3 Advent	(C)
Matthew				
1:1-17	A	W	4 Advent	—
4:1-11	B	W	1 Lent	A
5:13-20	B	W	Pr. 21	A
5:17-48	B	W	Pr. 22	A
6:7-15	A	W	Pr. 19	—
7:1-12	A	W	7 Epiphany	—
7:13-20	A	W	Pr. 4	—
8:1-13	A	W	Pr. 15	—
8:14-17, 28-34	A	W	3 Advent	—
8:23-27	A	W	Pr. 14	—
9:2-8	A	W	Pr. 21	—
9:14-17	A	W	2 Epiphany	—
9:27-34	A	W	4 Lent	—
10:5-23	A	W	Pr. 7	(A)
11:16-24	A	W	Pr. 8	(A)
12:1-8	A	W	Pr. 5	—
12:15-21	A	W	Baptism of Our Lord	—
12:22-32	A	W	Pr. 17	—
12:33-37	A	W	2 Advent	—
12:38-42	A	W	2 Easter	—
12:46-50	B	W	1 Christmas	—
13:10-17	A	W	Pr. 10	—
13:54-58	A	W	1 Christmas	—
15:1-9	B	W	Pr. 23	—
15:32-39	A	W	Pr. 13	—
17:14-21	B	W	Pr. 18	—

Daily reading		Year	Day	Week	RCL Occurrence
(Matt.)	17:22-27	A	W	Pr. 24	—
	18:6-14	A	W	1 Lent	A
	19:1-12	A	W	6 Epiphany	—
	19:16-22	A	W	Pr. 25	—
	19:23-30	A	W	Pr. 20	—
	20:17-28	A	W	4 Easter	—
	20:29-34	C	W	Pr. 22	—
	21:18-22	A	W	Pr. 18	—
	22:23-33	A	W	5 Lent	—
	23:13-28	A	W	Pr. 26	—
	24:1-14	A	W	Pr. 27	—
	24:15-31	B	W	1 Advent	—
	24:23-35	A	W	1 Advent	—
	24:45-51	A	W	Pr. 28	—
	26:6-13	A	W	Pr. 16	—
	28:1-10	A	W	Easter	altA
Mark					
	3:7-12	B	W	5 Epiphany	—
	3:13-19	B	W	3 Epiphany	—
	4:1-20	B	W	Pr. 6	—
	4:21-25	B	W	Holy Trinity	—
	4:30-34	A	W	Pr. 12	B
	5:1-20	B	W	4 Epiphany	—
	6:35-44	B	W	Pr. 12	—
	6:45-52	B	W	Pr. 7	—
	7:9-23	B	W	Pr. 17	(B)
	8:1-10	B	W	Pr. 13	—
	8:14-21	B	W	Pr. 15	—
	8:22-26	B	W	Pr. 25	—
	9:9-13	B	W	3 Advent	(B)
	9:14-2	B	W	Pr. 8	—
	10:32-34	B	W	2 Lent	—
	11:1-11	B	W	4 Advent	B
	11:12-14, 20-24	B	W	Pr. 27	—
	11:15-19	B	W	3 Lent	—
	11:27-33	B	W	2 Advent	—
	12:18-27	B	W	2 Easter	—
	13:9-23	B	W	Pr. 28	—
	14:26-31	B	W	4 Easter	B
	16:1-8	B	W	Easter	altB
	16:9-18	B	W	3 Easter	—
	16:19-20	B	W	6 Easter	—
Luke					
	1:5-25	C	W	4 Advent	—
	1:26-38	C	W	Pentecost	B

Daily reading		Year	Day	Week	RCL Occurrence
(Luke)	1:46-55	A	Sa	4 Advent	altABC
	1:46-55	C	W	Holy Trinity	altABC
	1:46-55	C	W	Pr. 25	altABC
	1:57-80	B	W	Pr. 10	—
	1:67-79	A	W	3 Epiphany	C
	1:67-79	C	Jan 9		C
	2:1-20	A	Dec 26		altABC
	2:1-20	B	Dec 26		altABC
	2:1-20	C	Dec 26		altABC
	2:25-38	C	W	6 Easter	B
	3:23-28	C	Dec 27		—
	4:31-37	C	W	Pr. 4	—
	4:38-44	C	W	3 Epiphany	—
	5:1-11	C	W	3 Easter	C
	5:12-16	C	W	Pr. 23	—
	5:17-26	C	W	Pr. 6	—
	5:27-32	C	W	5 Epiphany	—
	5:33-39	C	W	2 Epiphany	—
	6:1-11	C	W	Pr. 16	—
	6:12-19	A	W	Pr. 6	(C)
	6:17-26	A	W	4 Epiphany	C
	7:18-30	C	W	2 Advent	—
	7:31-35	C	W	3 Advent	—
	8:4-10	C	W	Pr. 11	—
	8:16-21	C	W	1 Christmas	—
	8:22-25	C	W	Pr. 12	—
	8:40-56	C	W	Pr. 5	—
	9:1-6	C	W	Pr. 9	—
	9:10-17	C	W	4 Lent	—
	9:18-27	C	W	7 Easter	—
	9:21-27	C	W	Pr. 8	—
	9:37-43	C	W	Pr. 7	C
	9:43b-48	C	W	Pr. 21	—
	10:21-24	C	T	Transfiguration	—
	10:25-28	C	W	5 Easter	—
	11:14-28	B	W	Pr. 5	—
	11:29-32	C	W	1 Advent	—
	11:33-36	C	W	Baptism of Our Lord	—
	11:37-52	C	W	6 Epiphany	—
	12:4-12	C	W	2 Easter	—
	12:22-31	A	W	8 Epiphany	—
	12:22-31	C	W	Pr. 13	—
	12:41-48	C	W	Pr. 14	—
	13:18-21	C	W	3 Lent	—
	13:22-31	C	W	2 Lent	—
	13:31-35	A	Jan 9		altC
	14:15-24	C	W	Pr. 17	—

Daily reading		Year	Day	Week	RCL Occurrence
(Luke)	14:34-35	C	W	8 Epiphany	—
	15:1-7	B	W	Pr. 11	C
	17:1-4	C	W	5 Epiphany	—
	17:20-37	C	W	Pr. 28	—
	18:15-17	B	W	2 Epiphany	—
	18:15-17	C	W	Christ the King	—
	18:18-30	C	W	Pr. 18	—
	18:31-34	C	W	5 Lent	—
	19:11-27	C	W	Pr. 26	—
	19:41-44	C	W	4 Epiphany	—
	19:45-48	C	W	Pr. 15	—
	20:1-8	C	W	Pr. 27	—
	20:45—21:4	C	W	Pr. 20	—
	21:34—22:6	C	W	1 Lent	(C)
	22:31-33, 54-62	C	W	Pr. 19	C
	22:39-46	C	W	Pr. 24	C
	24:1-12	C	W	Easter	altC
John					
	1:29-34	B	W	Baptism of Our Lord	A
	3:16-21	C	W	Pr. 10	(A)B
	3:22-36	B	W	8 Epiphany	—
	3:31-36	A	W	7 Easter	—
	4:46-54	B	W	6 Epiphany	—
	5:1-18	B	W	Pr. 4	(C)
	5:19-29	B	W	7 Epiphany	—
	5:19-40	A	W	Christ the King	—
	6:25-35	A	W	Pr. 23	B
	6:35-40	B	W	Pr. 14	(B)
	7:1-9	B	W	Pr. 9	—
	7:14-31, 37-39	A	W	3 Lent	(altA)
	7:25-39	B	W	Pr. 19	(altA)
	7:37-39	A	W	Pentecost	(altA)
	7:37-39	B	W	Pentecost	(altA)
	7:40-52	A	W	Pr. 22	—
	8:1-11	A	W	2 Lent	—
	8:12-30	A	W	5 Epiphany	—
	8:21-30	A	F	6 Easter	—
	8:21-38	B	W	Pr. 20	—
	8:31-38	A	W	5 Easter	—
	8:39-59	B	Jan 9		—
	10:31-42	C	W	4 Easter	—
	12:1-11	A	M	Passion	(C)
	12:20-36	A	T	Passion	(B)
	12:34-50	B	W	5 Lent	—
	13:1-17	A	W	Pr. 9	ABC

Daily reading		Year	Day	Week	RCL Occurrence
(John)	13:1-17	B	W	Pr. 24	ABC
	13:21-32	A	W	Passion	(ABC)
	13:31-35	B	W	Pr. 26	C
	14:15-31	A	W	Holy Trinity	(A altC)
	14:18-31	B	W	5 Easter	(A altC)
	15:16-25	B	W	Pr. 16	(B)
	16:16-24	B	W	7 Easter	—
	16:25-33	B	W	Christ the King	—
	21:1-14	A	W	3 Easter	C
	21:24-25	C	Sa	Christ the King	—
Acts					
	2:37-47	A	F	Pr. 13	(A)
	3:1-10	C	F	Pr. 4	—
	3:17—4:4	B	F	3 Advent	(B)
	4:13-31	B	F	Pr. 21	—
	5:12-16	A	F	3 Advent	—
	6:1-7	B	F	Pr. 15	—
	6:8-15	A	Th	5 Easter	—
	7:44-60	A	F	5 Easter	(A)
	8:4-13	A	F	Baptism of Our Lord	—
	8:26-40	A	F	2 Epiphany	B
	9:1-20	A	F	4 Lent	(C)
	11:1-18	B	F	2 Advent	C
	11:19-30	C	Th	3 Easter	—
	12:1-19	C	M	3 Easter	—
	13:16-33a	A	F	2 Advent	—
	13:42-52	B	F	1 Christmas	—
	14:8-18	B	F	7 Epiphany	—
	15:1-21	A	Th	Pr. 15	—
	15:1-5, 22-35	B	F	Pr. 4	—
	17:1-9	C	F	Pr. 16	—
	17:32—18:11	A	W	6 Easter	—
	19:21-41	C	F	Pr. 9	—
	20:16-38	B	F	Pr. 11	—
	21:27-39	B	Th	Pr. 10	—
	22:2-16	B	F	Baptism of Our Lord	—
	23:12-35	B	F	Pr. 10	—
	24:10-23	C	F	Pr. 27	—
	26:1, 12-29	C	T	3 Easter	—
	27:13-38	B	F	Pr. 7	—
	28:23-31	C	F	3 Advent	—
Romans					
	2:1-16	C	F	3 Lent	—
	3:9-22a	A	F	Pr. 4	—

Daily reading		Year	Day	Week	RCL Occurrence
(Rom.)	4:1-12	C	F	2 Lent	(A)
	4:6-13	A	F	2 Lent	(A)
	7:1-20	A	F	Pr. 9	(A)
	8:14-27	A	F	Pentecost	B
	8:18-30	C	F	4 Advent	(AB)
	9:14-29	A	F	Pr. 14	—
	9:30—10:4	A	F	Pr. 16	—
	11:13-29	A	F	Pr. 15	(A)
	12:9-21	A	F	7 Epiphany	A
	13:1-7	A	F	Pr. 18	—
	14:13—15:2	A	F	Pr. 19	—
	16:1-20	A	F	Pr. 20	—
1 Corinthians					
	1:3-17	C	F	2 Epiphany	(A)
	2:1-13	C	F	Pentecost	A
	3:10-23	B	F	3 Lent	(A)
	4:6-21	A	F	8 Epiphany	—
	7:1-16	B	F	Pr. 22	—
	7:17-24	B	F	3 Epiphany	—
	7:32-40	B	F	4 Epiphany	—
	9:1-16	B	F	5 Epiphany	—
	10:14—11:1	B	F	6 Epiphany	—
	11:2-22, 27-33	C	F	7 Epiphany	—
	12:1-13	A	F	Holy Trinity	C altA
	12:4-27	B	F	Pentecost	(C altA)
	14:1-12	C	F	3 Epiphany	—
	14:13-25	C	F	4 Epiphany	—
	14:26-40	C	F	5 Epiphany	—
	15:12-28	A	F	2 Easter	(C)
	15:20-34	C	F	6 Epiphany	(C)
	15:35-58	B	F	Easter	(C)
	16:1-24	C	F	8 Epiphany	—
2 Corinthians					
	1:1-11	B	F	7 Epiphany	—
	1:23—2:11	B	F	8 Epiphany	—
	3:4-11	B	F	5 Lent	(B)
	4:1-12	A	F	5 Epiphany	(BC)
	6:14—7:1	B	F	2 Epiphany	—
	7:2-16	B	F	Pr. 8	—
	9:1-19	C	F	Pr. 20	—
	11:16-33	B	F	Pr. 9	—
Galatians					
	2:1-14	C	F	Pr. 5	—
	3:1-14	C	F	Pr. 6	—

Daily reading	Year	Day	Week	RCL Occurrence
(Gal.) 3:15-22	C	F	Pr. 7	—
3:23—4:7	A	F	4 Advent	BC (Jan 1)
4:8-20	C	F	Pr. 8	—
4:21—5:1	A	F	Pr. 11	(C)
5:16-26	B	F	5 Easter	C
Ephesians				
2:1-10	A	F	5 Lent	B
2:11-22	B	Jan 11		B
3:14-21	A	Jan 11		B
4:1-16	C	F	Holy Trinity	B
4:17-24	B	F	Pr. 13	(B)
4:17—5:1	C	Jan 11		(B)
4:17—5:2	A	F	Pr. 10	(B)
5:1-14	B	F	Pr. 14	(A)
5:21—6:9	B	F	Pr. 16	—
6:10-18	A	F	Pr. 12	B
Philippians				
1:3-30	A	F	Pr. 21	(C)
2:12-18	A	F	3 Epiphany	—
3:13—4:1	A	F	Pr. 23	(C)
4:10-20	B	F	Pr. 12	—
Colossians				
1:27—2:7	C	F	Pr. 11	(C)
2:16—3:1	C	F	Pr. 12	(C)
3:1-17	A	F	Easter	C
3:18—4:5	C	F	Pr. 13	—
1 Thessalonians				
2:13-20	A	F	Pr. 26	(A)
3:6-13	A	F	Pr. 27	(C)
4:1-12; 5:12-18	A	F	Pr. 28	(B)
4:1-18	B	F	1 Advent	(A)
2 Thessalonians				
1:3-12	C	F	Pr. 28	(C)
2:13—3:5	A	F	Pr. 6	(C)
1 Timothy				
1:1-11	C	F	Pr. 19	—
3:11—4:16	C	F	Pr. 18	—
2 Timothy				
2:1-7	C	F	Pr. 23	—
2:14-26	C	F	Pr. 24	(C)

Daily reading		Year	Day	Week	RCL Occurrence
(2 Tim.)	3:1-15	C	F	Pr. 25	(C)
Titus					
	2:11—3:7	A	Dec 31		altABC
	2:11—3:7	B	Dec 31		altABC
Philemon					
	1-25	A	F	4 Epiphany	(C)
Hebrews					
	1:1—2:4	C	Dec 31		(ABC)
	3:1-6	B	F	4 Lent	—
	3:7—4:7	B	F	Pr. 23	—
	4:4—5:14	A	F	1 Lent	(B)
	6:1-20	B	F	Pr. 24	—
	7:1-22	B	F	Pr. 25	—
	8:1-13	B	F	4 Advent	—
	9:1-12	B	F	Pr. 26	(B)
	9:1-14	C	F	1 Christmas	(B)
	9:15-24	B	F	Pr. 27	—
	10:26-39	B	F	Pr. 28	—
	10:26-39	C	F	Pr. 15	—
	11:1-3, 8-19	B	F	2 Lent	(C)
	11:1-7, 17-28	C	F	Pr. 14	(C)
	11:23-28, 32-40	A	F	1 Christmas	(C)
	11:1-7, 32-40	A	F	1 Advent	(C)
	11:29—12:2	B	F	Pr. 18	C
	12:3-17	C	F	Pr. 16	—
	13:1-16	A	F	Pr. 5	(C)
	13:7-21	C	F	Pr. 17	(C)
James					
	1:1-16	B	F	Pr. 17	—
	2:1-13	A	F	6 Epiphany	B
	2:8-26	A	F	Pr. 25	(B)
	2:14-26	C	F	Pr. 10	(B)
	2:17-26	B	F	Pr. 19	(B)
	4:8—5:6	B	F	Pr. 20	—
1 Peter					
	1:8-16	A	F	3 Easter	(A)
	2:4-10	A	F	Pr. 22	A
	2:9-17	A	F	4 Easter	(A)
	3:8-18a	B	F	1 Lent	(A)
	3:21—4:11	A	F	7 Easter	(A)

Daily reading		Year	Day	Week	RCL Occurrence
(1 Peter)	5:1-5	B	F	4 Easter	—
2 Peter					
	1:2-15	C	F	2 Advent	—
	2:4-21	C	F	1 Lent	—
	3:14-18	C	F	1 Advent	(B)
1 John					
	2:3-17	B	F	2 Easter	—
	2:18-28	C	F	5 Lent	—
	3:7-15	B	F	3 Easter	(B)
	4:1-6	A	F	Pr. 8	—
	5:13-21	C	F	Baptism of Our Lord	(B)
2 John					
	1-13	A	F	3 Lent	—
3 John					
	1-15	B	F	7 Easter	—
Jude					
	5-21	C	F	Pr. 26	—
Revelation					
	1:9-18	B	F	6 Easter	—
	1:9-18	C	F	2 Easter	—
	2:1-11	A	F	Pr. 7	—
	2:12-29	C	F	Pr. 22	—
	3:1-13	A	F	Pr. 17	—
	3:14-22	C	F	Pr. 21	—
	4:1-11	B	F	Holy Trinity	—
	5:1-10	C	F	3 Easter	—
	6:1—7:3	C	F	4 Easter	—
	10:1-11	C	F	5 Easter	—
	11:15-19	B	F	Christ the King	—
	12:1-12	C	F	Easter	—
	12:13-17	C	F	6 Easter	—
	14:12-20	A	W	Pr. 11	—
	18:1-10, 19-20	A	F	Pr. 24	—
	19:1-9	A	F	Christ the King	—
	19:1-9	C	F	4 Lent	—
	19:9-21	C	F	7 Easter	—
	20:1-15	B	F	Pr. 5	—
	21:5-27	C	F	Christ the King	(C Jan1)
	21:22—22:5	B	F	Pr. 6	C

Index to Sunday and Festival Readings

Sunday and major festival readings are drawn from the Revised Common Lectionary (RCL); lesser festival readings reflect ecumenical usage. During the season after Pentecost, the Old Testament selections without an asterisk are thematically related to the gospel; the alternate selections, marked with an asterisk (*), form a semi-continuous pattern of readings. Either series is intended to be read in its entirety.

RCL | Lesser Festival reading	Year	RCL* | Lesser Festival
Genesis		
1:1—2:4a	A	Holy Trinity
1:1—2:4a	ABC	Vigil of Easter
1:1-5	B	Baptism of Our Lord
1:1-5, 26-31	ABC	St. John
2:15-17; 3:1-7	A	1 Lent
2:18-24	B	S. btwn. Oct. 2 and 8, Pr. 22
3:8-15	B	S. btwn. June 5 and 11, Pr. 5
6:9-22; 7:24; 8:14-19	A	S. btwn. May 29 and June 4, Pr. 4*
7:1-5, 11-18; 8:6-18; 9:8-13	ABC	Vigil of Easter
9:8-17	B	1 Lent
11:1-9	C	Day of Pentecost
12:1-4a	A	2 Lent
12:1-9	A	S. btwn. June 5 and 11, Pr. 5*
15:1-6	C	S. btwn. Aug. 7 and 13, Pr. 14
15:1-12, 17-18	C	2 Lent
17:1-7, 15-16	B	2 Lent
18:1-10a	C	S. btwn. July 17 and 23, Pr. 11
18:1-15 [21:1-7]	A	S. btwn. June 12 and 18, Pr. 6*
18:20-32	C	S. btwn. July 24 and 30, Pr. 12
21:8-21	A	S. btwn. June 19 and 25, Pr. 7
22:1-14	A	S. btwn. June 26 and July 2, Pr. 8*
22:1-18	ABC	Vigil of Easter
24:34-38, 42-49, 58-67	A	S. btwn. July 3 and 9, Pr. 9*
25:19-34	A	S. btwn. July 10 and 16, Pr. 10*
28:10-19a	A	S. btwn. July 17 and 23, Pr. 11*
29:15-28	A	S. btwn. July 24 and 30, Pr. 12*
32:22-31	A	S. btwn. July 31 and Aug. 6, Pr. 13*
32:22-31	C	S. btwn. Oct. 16 and 22, Pr. 24
37:1-4, 12-28	A	S. btwn. Aug. 7 and 13, Pr. 14*
45:1-15	A	S. btwn. Aug. 14 and 20, Pr. 15*
45:3-11, 15	C	7 Epiphany
50:15-21	A	S. btwn. Sept. 11 and 17, Pr. 19

RCL	Lesser Festival reading	Year	RCL*	Lesser Festival
Exodus		
1:8—2:10	A	S. btwn. Aug. 21 and 27, Pr. 16*
2:1-10	ABC	St. Mary Magdalene
3:1-15	A	S. btwn. Aug. 28 and Sept. 3, Pr. 17*
12:1-14	A	S. btwn. Sept. 4 and 10, Pr. 18*
12:1-4 [5-10] 11-14	ABC	Maundy Thursday
14:10-31; 15:20-21	ABC	Vigil of Easter
14:19-31	A	S. btwn. Sept. 11 and 17, Pr. 19*
15:1b-11, 20-21	A	S. btwn. Sept. 11 and 17, Pr. 19*
15:1b-13, 17-18	ABC	Vigil of Easter
16:2-4, 9-15	B	S. btwn. July 31 and Aug. 6, Pr. 13
16:2-15	A	S. btwn. Sept. 18 and 24, Pr. 20*
17:1-7	A	3 Lent
17:1-7	A	S. btwn. Sept. 25 and Oct. 1, Pr. 21*
19:1-6	ABC	St. Bartholomew
19:1-9	ABC	Vigil of Pentecost
19:2-8a	A	S. btwn. June 12 and 18, Pr. 6
20:1-4, 7-9, 12-20	A	S. btwn. Oct. 2 and 8, Pr. 22*
20:1-17	B	3 Lent
24:12-18	A	Transfiguration of Our Lord
32:1-14	A	S. btwn. Oct. 9 and 15, Pr. 23*
32:7-14	C	S. btwn. Sept. 11 and 17, Pr. 19
33:12-23	A	S. btwn. Oct. 16 and 22, Pr. 24*
34:29-35	C	Transfiguration of Our Lord
Leviticus		
19:1-2, 9-18	A	7 Epiphany
19:1-2, 15-18	A	S. btwn. Oct. 23 and 29, Pr. 25
Numbers		
6:22-27	ABC	Name of Jesus
11:4-6, 10-16, 24-29	B	S. btwn. Sept. 25 and Oct. 1, Pr. 21
11:24-30	A	Day of Pentecost
21:4-9	B	4 Lent
21:4b-9	ABC	Holy Cross Day
Deuteronomy		
4:1-2, 6-9	B	S. btwn. Aug. 28 and Sept. 3, Pr. 17
5:12-15	B	S. btwn. May 29 and June 4, Pr. 4
6:1-9	B	S. btwn. Oct. 30 and Nov. 5, Pr. 2*
8:7-18	A	Thanksgiving Day
11:18-21, 26-28	A	S. btwn. May 29 and June 4, Pr. 4
18:15-20	B	4 Epiphany
26:1-11	C	1 Lent
26:1-11	C	Thanksgiving Day
30:9-14	C	S. btwn. July 10 and 16, Pr. 10

RCL | Lesser Festival reading	Year	RCL* | Lesser Festival
(Deut.) 30:15-20	A	6 Epiphany
30:15-20	C	S. btwn. Sept. 4 and 10, Pr. 18
31:19-30	ABC	Vigil of Easter
32:1-4, 7, 36a, 43a	ABC	Vigil of Easter
34:1-12	A	S. btwn. Oct. 23 and 29, Pr. 25*
Joshua		
3:7-17	A	S. btwn. Oct. 30 and Nov. 5, Pr. 26*
5:9-12	C	4 Lent
24:1-2a, 14-18	B	S. btwn. Aug. 21 and 27, Pr. 16
24:1-3a, 14-25	A	S. btwn. Nov. 6 and 12, Pr. 27*
Judges		
4:1-7	A	S. btwn. Nov. 13 and 19, Pr. 28*
6:36-40	ABC	St. Thomas
Ruth		
1:1-18	B	S. btwn. Oct. 30 and Nov. 5, Pr. 26*
1:6-18	ABC	St. Mary Magdalene
3:1-5; 4:13-17	B	S. btwn. Nov. 6 and 12, Pr. 27*
1 Samuel		
1:4-20	B	S. btwn. Nov. 13 and 19, Pr. 28*
2:1-10	B	S. btwn. Nov. 13 and 19, Pr. 28*
2:1-10	ABC	Visitation
2:18-20, 26	C	1 Christmas
3:1-10 [11-20]	B	2 Epiphany
3:1-10 [11-20]	B	S. btwn. May 29 and June 4, Pr. 4*
8:4-11 [12-15] 16-20 [11:14-15]	B	S. btwn. June 5 and 11, Pr. 5*
15:34—16:13	B	S. btwn. June 12 and 18, Pr. 6*
16:1-13	A	4 Lent
17:[1a, 4-11, 19-23] 32-49	B	S. btwn. June 19 and 25, Pr. 7*
17:57—18:5, 10-16	B	S. btwn. June 19 and 25, Pr. 7*
2 Samuel		
1:1, 17-27	B	S. btwn. June 26 and July 2, Pr. 8*
5:1-5, 9-10	B	S. btwn. July 3 and 9, Pr. 9*
6:1-5, 12b-19	B	S. btwn. July 10 and 16, Pr. 10*
7:1-11, 16	B	4 Advent
7:1-14a	B	S. btwn. July 17 and 23, Pr. 11*
11:1-15	B	S. btwn. July 24 and 30, Pr. 12*
11:26—12:10, 13-15	C	S. btwn. June 12 and 18, Pr. 6*
11:26—12:13a	B	S. btwn. July 31 and Aug. 6, Pr. 13*
18:5-9, 15, 31-33	B	S. btwn. Aug. 7 and 13, Pr. 14*
23:1-7	B	Christ the King, Pr. 29*

RCL	Lesser Festival reading	Year	RCL*	Lesser Festival
1 Kings		
2:10-12; 3:3-14	B	S. btwn. Aug. 14 and 20, Pr. 15*
3:5-12	A	S. btwn. July 24 and 30, Pr. 12
8:[1, 6, 10-11] 22-30, 41-43	B	S. btwn. Aug. 21 and 27, Pr. 16*
8:22-23, 41-43	C	S. btwn. May 29 and June 4, Pr. 4*
17:8-16	B	S. btwn. Nov. 6 and 12, Pr. 27
17:8-16 [17-24]	C	S. btwn. June 5 and 11, Pr. 5*
17:17-24	C	S. btwn. June 5 and 11, Pr. 5
18:20-21 [22-29] 30-39	C	S. btwn. May 29 and June 4, Pr. 4*
19:1-4 [5-7] 8-15a	C	S. btwn. June 19 and 25, Pr. 7*
19:4-8	B	S. btwn. Aug. 7 and 13, Pr. 14
19:9-18	A	S. btwn. Aug. 7 and 13, Pr. 14
19:9-18	ABC	St. James the Elder
19:15-16, 19-21	C	S. btwn. June 26 and July 2, Pr. 8
21:1-10 [11-14] 15-21a	C	S. btwn. June 12 and 18, Pr. 6*
2 Kings		
2:1-12	B	Transfiguration of Our Lord
2:1-2, 6-14	C	S. btwn. June 26 and July 2, Pr. 8
4:42-44	B	S. btwn. July 24 and 30, Pr. 12
5:1-3, 7-15c	C	S. btwn. Oct. 9 and 15, Pr. 23
5:1-14	B	6 Epiphany
5:1-14	C	S. btwn. July 3 and 9, Pr. 9
2 Chronicles		
24:17-22	ABC	St. Stephen
Nehemiah		
8:1-3, 5-6, 8-10	C	3 Epiphany
Esther		
7:1-6, 9-10; 9:20-22	B	S. btwn. Sept. 25 and Oct. 1, Pr. 21*
Job		
1:1; 2:1-10	B	S. btwn. Oct. 2 and 8, Pr. 22*
14:1-14	ABC	Holy Saturday
19:23-27a	C	S. btwn. Nov. 6 and 12, Pr. 27
23:1-9, 16-17	B	S. btwn. Oct. 9 and 15, Pr. 23*
38:1-7 [34-41]	B	S. btwn. Oct. 16 and 22, Pr. 24*
38:1-11	B	S. btwn. June 19 and 25, Pr. 7
42:1-6, 10-17	B	S. btwn. Oct. 23 and 29, Pr. 25*
Psalms		
1	C	6 Epiphany
1	B	7 Easter

RCL | Lesser Festival reading		Year	RCL* | Lesser Festival
(Ps.)	1	C	S. btwn. Sept. 4 and 10, Pr. 18
	1	B	S. btwn. Sept. 18 and 24, Pr. 20*
	1	A	S. btwn. Oct. 23 and 29, Pr. 25
	2	A	Transfiguration of Our Lord
	4	B	3 Easter
	5:1-8	C	S. btwn. June 12 and 18, Pr. 6*
	7:1-10	ABC	St. James the Elder
	8	A, C	Holy Trinity
	8	ABC	Name of Jesus
	8	ABC	New Year's Eve
	8	B	S. btwn. Oct. 2 and 8, Pr. 22
	9:9-20	B	S. btwn. June 19 and 25, Pr. 7*
	11	ABC	St. Simon and St. Jude
	12	ABC	St. Bartholomew
	13	A	S. btwn. June 26 and July 2, Pr. 8*
	14	B	S. btwn. July 24 and 30, Pr. 12*
	14	C	S. btwn. Sept. 11 and 17, Pr. 19*
	15	A	4 Epiphany
	15	B	S. btwn. Aug. 28 and Sept. 3, Pr. 17
	15	C	S. btwn. July 17 and 23, Pr. 11
	16	A	2 Easter
	16	C	S. btwn. June 26 and July 2, Pr. 8
	16	B	S. btwn. Nov. 13 and 19, Pr. 28
	16	ABC	Vigil of Easter
	17:1-7, 15	A	S. btwn. July 31 and Aug. 6, Pr. 13*
	17:1-9	C	S. btwn. Nov. 6 and 12, Pr. 27
	17:1-9, 15	ABC	St. Stephen
	18:1-6, 16-19	ABC	Confession of St. Peter
	19	C	3 Epiphany
	19	B	3 Lent
	19	A	S. btwn. Oct. 2 and 8, Pr. 22*
	19	B	S. btwn. Sept. 11 and 17, Pr. 19*
	19	ABC	Vigil of Easter
	19:1-6	ABC	St. Andrew
	19:7-14	B	S. btwn. Sept. 25 and Oct. 1, Pr. 21
	20	B	S. btwn. June 12 and 18, Pr. 6*
	22	ABC	Good Friday
	22:1-15	B	S. btwn. Oct. 9 and 15, Pr. 23*
	22:19-28	C	S. btwn. June 19 and 25, Pr. 7*
	22:23-31	B	2 Lent
	22:25-31	B	5 Easter
	23	ABC	4 Easter
	23	A	4 Lent
	23	B	S. btwn. July 17 and 23, Pr. 11*
	23	A	S. btwn. Oct. 9 and 15, Pr. 23*
	24	B	All Saints Day

RCL | Lesser Festival reading	Year	RCL* | Lesser Festival
(Ps.) 24	B	S. btwn. July 10 and 16, Pr. 10*
24:7-10	ABC	Presentation of Our Lord
25:1-9	A	S. btwn. Sept. 25 and Oct. 1, Pr. 21
25:1-10	C	1 Advent
25:1-10	B	1 Lent
25:1-10	C	S. btwn. July 10 and 16, Pr. 10*
26	B	S. btwn. Oct. 2 and 8, Pr. 22
26:1-8	A	S. btwn. Aug. 28 and Sept. 3, Pr. 17
27	C	2 Lent
27:1, 4-9	A	3 Epiphany
29	ABC	Baptism of Our Lord
29	B	Holy Trinity
30	C	3 Easter
30	B	6 Epiphany
30	C	S. btwn. July 3 and 9, Pr. 9*
30	B	S. btwn. June 26 and July 2, Pr. 8
30	C	S. btwn. June 5 and 11, Pr. 5
31:1-4, 15-16	ABC	Holy Saturday
31:1-5, 15-16	A	5 Easter
31:1-5, 19-24	A	S. btwn. May 29 and June 4, Pr. 4
31:9-16	ABC	Sunday of the Passion
32	A	1 Lent
32	C	4 Lent
32	C	S. btwn. June 12 and 18, Pr. 6
32:1-7	C	S. btwn. Oct. 30 and Nov. 5, Pr. 26
33:1-12	A	S. btwn. June 5 and 11, Pr. 5*
33:12-22	C	S. btwn. Aug. 7 and 13, Pr. 14
33:12-22	ABC	Vigil of Pentecost
34:1-8	B	S. btwn. Aug. 7 and 13, Pr. 14
34:1-8 [19-22]	B	S. btwn. Oct. 23 and 29, Pr. 25*
34:1-10, 22	A	All Saints Day
34:9-14	B	S. btwn. Aug. 14 and 20, Pr. 15
34:15-22	B	S. btwn. Aug. 21 and 27, Pr. 16
36:5-10	C	2 Epiphany
36:5-11	ABC	Monday after Passion Sunday
37:1-9	C	S. btwn. Oct. 2 and 8, Pr. 22
37:1-11, 39-40	C	7 Epiphany
40:1-11	A	2 Epiphany
40:5-10	ABC	Annunciation of Our Lord
41	B	7 Epiphany
42 and 43	C	S. btwn. June 19 and 25, Pr. 7*
42 and 43	ABC	Vigil of Easter
43	A	S. btwn. Oct. 30 and Nov. 5, Pr. 26
43	C	Vigil of Easter
44:1-3, 20-26	ABC	St. Philip and St. James
45	ABC	Annunciation of Our Lord

RCL | Lesser Festival reading		Year	RCL* | Lesser Festival
(Ps.)	45:1-2, 6-9	B	S. btwn. Aug. 28 and Sept. 3, Pr. 17*
	45:10-15	ABC	Mary, Mother of Our Lord
	45:10-17	A	S. btwn. July 3 and 9, Pr. 9*
	46	C	Christ the King, Pr. 29
	46	ABC	Reformation Day
	46	A	S. btwn. May 29 and June 4, Pr. 4*
	46	ABC	Vigil of Easter
	47	ABC	Ascension of Our Lord
	48	B	S. btwn. July 3 and 9, Pr. 9*
	49:1-12	C	S. btwn. July 31 and Aug. 6, Pr. 13
	50:1-6	B	Transfiguration of Our Lord
	50:1-8, 22-23	C	S. btwn. Aug. 7 and 13, Pr. 14*
	50:7-15	A	S. btwn. June 5 and 11, Pr. 5
	51:1-10	C	S. btwn. Sept. 11 and 17, Pr. 19
	51:1-12	B	5 Lent
	51:1-12	B	S. btwn. July 31 and Aug. 6, Pr. 13*
	51:1-17	ABC	Ash Wednesday
	52	C	S. btwn. July 17 and 23, Pr. 11*
	54	B	S. btwn. Sept. 18 and 24, Pr. 20
	56	ABC	St. Matthias
	57	ABC	St. Mark
	62:5-12	B	3 Epiphany
	63:1-8	C	3 Lent
	65	C	S. btwn. Oct. 23 and 29, Pr. 25*
	65	A	Thanksgiving Day
	65:[1-8] 9-13	A	S. btwn. July 10 and 16, Pr. 10
	66:1-9	C	S. btwn. July 3 and 9, Pr. 9
	66:1-12	C	S. btwn. Oct. 9 and 15, Pr. 23*
	66:8-20	A	6 Easter
	67	C	6 Easter
	67	ABC	Conversion of St. Paul
	67	A	S. btwn. Aug. 14 and 20, Pr. 15
	68:1-10, 32-35	A	7 Easter
	69:7-10 [11-15] 16-18	A	S. btwn. June 19 and 25, Pr. 7
	70	A	S. btwn. Nov. 6 and 12, Pr. 27
	70	ABC	Wednesday after Passion Sunday
	71:1-6	C	4 Epiphany
	71:1-6	C	S. btwn. Aug. 21 and 27, Pr. 16*
	71:1-14	ABC	Tuesday after Passion Sunday
	72:1-7, 10-14	ABC	Epiphany of Our Lord
	72:1-7, 18-19	A	2 Advent
	73:23-28	ABC	St. Mary Magdalene
	77:1-2, 11-20	C	S. btwn. June 26 and July 2, Pr. 8*
	78:1-2, 34-38	ABC	Holy Cross Day
	78:1-4, 12-16	A	S. btwn. Sept. 25 and Oct. 1, Pr. 21*
	78:1-7	A	S. btwn. Nov. 6 and 12, Pr. 27*

RCL | Lesser Festival reading	Year	RCL* | Lesser Festival
(Ps.) 78:23-29	B	S. btwn. July 31 and Aug. 6, Pr. 13
79:1-9	C	S. btwn. Sept. 18 and 24, Pr. 20*
80:1-2, 8-19	C	S. btwn. Aug. 14 and 20, Pr. 15*
80:1-7	C	4 Advent
80:1-7, 17-19	B	1 Advent
80:1-7, 17-19	A	4 Advent
80:7-15	A	S. btwn. Oct. 2 and 8, Pr. 22
81:1, 10-16	C	S. btwn. Aug. 28 and Sept. 3, Pr. 17*
81:1-10	B	S. btwn. May 29 and June 4, Pr. 4
82	C	S. btwn. Aug. 14 and 20, Pr. 15
82	C	S. btwn. July 10 and 16, Pr. 10*
84	ABC	Presentation of Our Lord
84	B	S. btwn. Aug. 21 and 27, Pr. 16*
84:1-7	C	S. btwn. Oct. 23 and 29, Pr. 25
85	C	S. btwn. July 24 and 30, Pr. 12*
85:1-2, 8-13	B	2 Advent
85:8-13	A	S. btwn. Aug. 7 and 13, Pr. 14
85:8-13	B	S. btwn. July 10 and 16, Pr. 10
86:1-10, 16-17	A	S. btwn. June 19 and 25, Pr. 7*
86:11-17	A	S. btwn. July 17 and 23, Pr. 11
87:1-2, 4-6	ABC	St. Peter and St. Paul
89:1-4, 15-18	A	S. btwn. June 26 and July 2, Pr. 8
89:1-4, 19-26	B	4 Advent
89:20-37	B	S. btwn. July 17 and 23, Pr. 11*
90:1-6, 13-17	A	S. btwn. Oct. 23 and 29, Pr. 25*
90:1-8 [9-11] 12	A	S. btwn. Nov. 13 and 19, Pr. 28
90:12-17	B	S. btwn. Oct. 9 and 15, Pr. 23
91:1-2, 9-16	C	1 Lent
91:1-6, 14-16	C	S. btwn. Sept. 25 and Oct. 1, Pr. 21*
91:9-16	B	S. btwn. Oct. 16 and 22, Pr. 24
92:1-4, 12-15	C	8 Epiphany
92:1-4, 12-15	B	S. btwn. June 12 and 18, Pr. 6
92:1-4, 12-15	C	S. btwn. May 24 and 28, Pr. 3
93	ABC	Ascension of Our Lord
93	B	Christ the King, Pr. 29
95	A	3 Lent
95:1-7a	A	Christ the King, Pr. 29
96	ABC	Christmas Eve (I)
96	C	S. btwn. May 29 and June 4, Pr. 4*
96:1-9	C	S. btwn. May 29 and June 4, Pr. 4
96:1-9 [10-13]	A	S. btwn. Oct. 16 and 22, Pr. 24
97	C	7 Easter
97	ABC	Christmas Dawn (II)
98	B	6 Easter
98	ABC	Christmas Day (III)
98	C	S. btwn. Nov. 13 and 19, Pr. 28

RCL | Lesser Festival reading	Year	RCL* | Lesser Festival
(Ps.) 98	C	S. btwn. Nov. 6 and 12, Pr. 27*
98	ABC	Vigil of Easter
98:1-5	ABC	Holy Cross Day
99	A	S. btwn. Oct. 16 and 22, Pr. 24*
99	A, C	Transfiguration of Our Lord
100	A	Christ the King, Pr. 29*
100	A	S. btwn. June 12 and 18, Pr. 6
100	C	Thanksgiving Day
103:1-5, 20-22	ABC	St. Michael and All Angels
103:[1-7] 8-13	A	S. btwn. Sept. 11 and 17, Pr. 19
103:1-8	C	S. btwn. Aug. 21 and 27, Pr. 16
103:1-13, 22	B	8 Epiphany
103:1-13, 22	B	S. btwn. May 24 and 28, Pr. 3
104:1-9, 24, 35c	B	S. btwn. Oct. 16 and 22, Pr. 24*
104:24-34, 35b	ABC	Day of Pentecost
105:1-11, 45b	A	S. btwn. July 24 and 30, Pr. 12*
105:1-6, 16-22, 45b	A	S. btwn. Aug. 7 and 13, Pr. 14*
105:1-6, 23-26, 45c	A	S. btwn. Aug. 28 and Sept. 3, Pr. 17*
105:1-6, 37-45	A	S. btwn. Sept. 18 and 24, Pr. 20*
106:1-6, 19-23	A	S. btwn. Oct. 9 and 15, Pr. 23*
107:1-3, 17-22	B	4 Lent
107:1-3, 23-32	B	S. btwn. June 19 and 25, Pr. 7
107:1-7, 33-37	A	S. btwn. Oct. 30 and Nov. 5, Pr. 26*
107:1-9, 43	C	S. btwn. July 31 and Aug. 6, Pr. 13
111	B	4 Epiphany
111	B	S. btwn. Aug. 14 and 20, Pr. 15*
111	C	S. btwn. Oct. 9 and 15, Pr. 23
112	C	S. btwn. Aug. 28 and Sept. 3, Pr. 17
112	ABC	St. Barnabas
112:1-9 [10]	A	5 Epiphany
113	C	S. btwn. Sept. 18 and 24, Pr. 20
113	ABC	Visitation
114	ABC	Easter Evening
114	A	S. btwn. Sept. 11 and 17, Pr. 19*
114	ABC	Vigil of Easter
116:1-2, 12-19	ABC	Maundy Thursday
116:1-2, 12-19	A	S. btwn. June 12 and 18, Pr. 6*
116:1-4, 12-19	A	3 Easter
116:1-9	B	S. btwn. Sept. 11 and 17, Pr. 19
116:12-19	ABC	St. John
118:1-2, 14-24	ABC	Easter Day
118:14-29	C	2 Easter
119:1-8	A	6 Epiphany
119:1-8	B	S. btwn. Oct. 30 and Nov. 5, Pr. 26
119:9-16	B	5 Lent
119:33-40	A	7 Epiphany

RCL | Lesser Festival reading	Year	RCL* | Lesser Festival
(Ps.) 119:33-40	A	S. btwn. Sept. 4 and 10, Pr. 18
119:33-40	ABC	St. Matthew
119:97-104	C	S. btwn. Oct. 16 and 22, Pr. 24*
119:105-112	A	S. btwn. July 10 and 16, Pr. 10*
119:129-136	A	S. btwn. July 24 and 30, Pr. 12
119:137-144	C	S. btwn. Oct. 30 and Nov. 5, Pr. 26*
121	A	2 Lent
121	C	S. btwn. Oct. 16 and 22, Pr. 24
122	A	1 Advent
123	B	S. btwn. July 3 and 9, Pr. 9
123	A	S. btwn. Nov. 13 and 19, Pr. 28*
124	ABC	Holy Innocents
124	A	S. btwn. Aug. 21 and 27, Pr. 16*
124	B	S. btwn. Sept. 25 and Oct. 1, Pr. 21*
124	ABC	St. Luke
125	B	S. btwn. Sept. 4 and 10, Pr. 18*
126	C	5 Lent
126	B	3 Advent
126	B	S. btwn. Oct. 23 and 29, Pr. 25
126	B	Thanksgiving Day
127	B	S. btwn. Nov. 6 and 12, Pr. 27*
128	A	S. btwn. July 24 and 30, Pr. 12*
130	A	5 Lent
130	B	S. btwn. Aug. 7 and 13, Pr. 14*
130	B	S. btwn. June 26 and July 2, Pr. 8*
130	B	S. btwn. June 5 and 11, Pr. 5
130	ABC	Vigil of Pentecost
131	A	8 Epiphany
131	A	S. btwn. May 24 and 28, Pr. 3
132:1-12 [13-18]	B	Christ the King, Pr. 29*
133	B	2 Easter
133	A	S. btwn. Aug. 14 and 20, Pr. 15*
133	B	S. btwn. June 19 and 25, Pr. 7*
136:1-4, 23-26	ABC	St. Thomas
136:1-9, 23-26	ABC	Vigil of Easter
137	C	S. btwn. Oct. 2 and 8, Pr. 22*
138	C	5 Epiphany
138	A	S. btwn. Aug. 21 and 27, Pr. 16
138	C	S. btwn. July 24 and 30, Pr. 12
138	B	S. btwn. June 5 and 11, Pr. 5*
139:1-6, 13-18	C	S. btwn. Sept. 4 and 10, Pr. 1*8
139:1-6, 13-18	B	2 Epiphany
139:1-6, 13-18	B	S. btwn. May 29 and June 4, Pr. 4*
139:1-12, 23-24	A	S. btwn. July 17 and 23, Pr. 11*
141	ABC	Nativity of St. John the Baptist
143	ABC	Vigil of Easter

RCL | Lesser Festival reading	Year	RCL* | Lesser Festival
(Ps.) 145:1-5, 17-21	C	S. btwn. Nov. 6 and 12, Pr. 27*
145:1-8	A	S. btwn. Sept. 18 and 24, Pr. 20
145:8-14	A	S. btwn. July 3 and 9, Pr. 9
145:8-9, 14-21	A	S. btwn. July 31 and Aug. 6, Pr. 13
145:10-18	B	S. btwn. July 24 and 30, Pr. 12
146	C	S. btwn. June 5 and 11, Pr. 5*
146	B	S. btwn. Nov. 6 and 12, Pr. 27
146	B	S. btwn. Oct. 30 and Nov. 5, Pr. 26*
146	C	S. btwn. Sept. 25 and Oct. 1, Pr. 21
146	B	S. btwn. Sept. 4 and 10, Pr. 18
146:5-10	A	3 Advent
147:1-11, 20c	B	5 Epiphany
147:12-20	ABC	2 Christmas
148	ABC	1 Christmas
148	C	5 Easter
149	C	All Saints Day
149	A	S. btwn. Sept. 4 and 10, Pr. 18*
150	C	2 Easter
Proverbs		
1:20-33	B	S. btwn. Sept. 11 and 17, Pr. 19*
8:1-4, 22-31	C	Holy Trinity
8:1-8, 19-21; 9:4b-6	ABC	Vigil of Easter
9:1-6	B	S. btwn. Aug. 14 and 20, Pr. 15
22:1-2, 8-9, 22-23	B	S. btwn. Sept. 4 and 10, Pr. 18*
25:6-7	C	S. btwn. Aug. 28 and Sept. 3, Pr. 17
31:10-31	B	S. btwn. Sept. 18 and 24, Pr. 20*
Ecclesiastes		
1:2, 12-14; 2:18-23	C	S. btwn. July 31 and Aug. 6, Pr. 13
3:1-13	ABC	New Year's Eve
Song of Solomon		
2:8-13	B	S. btwn. Aug. 28 and Sept. 3, Pr. 17*
2:8-13	A	S. btwn. July 3 and 9, Pr. 9*
Isaiah		
1:1, 10-20	C	S. btwn. Aug. 7 and 13, Pr. 14*
1:10-18	C	S. btwn. Oct. 30 and Nov. 5, Pr. 26
2:1-5	A	1 Advent
5:1-7	C	S. btwn. Aug. 14 and 20, Pr. 15*
5:1-7	A	S. btwn. Oct. 2 and 8, Pr. 22
6:1-8	B	Holy Trinity
6:1-8 [9-13]	C	5 Epiphany
7:10-14	ABC	Annunciation of Our Lord
7:10-16	A	4 Advent

RCL	Lesser Festival reading	Year	RCL*	Lesser Festival
(Isa.)	9:1-4	A		3 Epiphany
	9:2-7	ABC		Christmas Eve (I)
	11:1-10	A		2 Advent
	12	C		S. btwn. Nov. 13 and 19, Pr. 28*
	12:2-6	C		3 Advent
	12:2-6	ABC		Vigil of Easter
	25:1-9	A		S. btwn. Oct. 9 and 15, Pr. 23
	25:6-9	B		All Saints Day
	25:6-9	B		Easter Day
	25:6-9	ABC		Easter Evening
	30:18-21	ABC		St. Philip and St. James
	35:1-10	A		3 Advent
	35:4-7a	B		S. btwn. Sept. 4 and 10, Pr. 18
	35:5-8	ABC		St. Luke
	40:1-11	B		2 Advent
	40:21-31	B		5 Epiphany
	42:1-9	A		Baptism of Our Lord
	42:1-9	ABC		Monday after Passion Sunday
	42:5-12	ABC		St. Barnabas
	43:1-7	C		Baptism of Our Lord
	43:16-21	C		5 Lent
	43:18-25	B		7 Epiphany
	43:8-13	ABC		St. Luke
	44:6-8	A		S. btwn. July 17 and 23, Pr. 11
	45:1-7	A		S. btwn. Oct. 16 and 22, Pr. 24
	49:1-7	A		2 Epiphany
	49:1-7	ABC		Tuesday in Holy Week
	49:8-16a	A		8 Epiphany
	49:8-16a	A		S. btwn. May 24 and 28, Pr. 3
	50:4-9a	B		S. btwn. Sept. 11 and 17, Pr. 19
	50:4-9a	ABC		Sunday of the Passion
	50:4-9a	ABC		Wednesday in Holy Week
	51:1-6	A		S. btwn. Aug. 21 and 27, Pr. 16
	52:7-10	ABC		Christmas Day (III)
	52:7-10	ABC		St. Mark
	52:13—53:12	ABC		Good Friday
	53:4-12	B		S. btwn. Oct. 16 and 22, Pr. 24
	55:1-5	A		S. btwn. July 31 and Aug. 6, Pr. 13
	55:1-9	C		3 Lent
	55:1-11	ABC		Vigil of Easter
	55:10-13	A		S. btwn. July 10 and 16, Pr. 10
	55:10-13	C		S. btwn. May 24 and 28, Pr. 3
	55:10-13	C		8 Epiphany
	56:1, 6-8	A		S. btwn. Aug. 14 and 20, Pr. 15
	58:1-9a [9b-12]	A		5 Epiphany
	58:1-12	ABC		Ash Wednesday

RCL	Lesser Festival reading	Year	RCL*	Lesser Festival
(Isa.)	58:9b-14	C	S. btwn. Aug. 21 and 27, Pr. 16
	60:1-6	ABC	Epiphany of Our Lord
	61:1-4, 8-11	B	3 Advent
	61:10—62:3	B	1 Christmas
	61:7-11	ABC	Mary, Mother of Our Lord
	62:1-5	C	2 Epiphany
	62:6-12	ABC	Christmas Dawn (II)
	63:7-9	A	1 Christmas
	64:1-9	B	1 Advent
	65:1-9	C	S. btwn. June 19 and 25, Pr. 7
	65:17-25	C	Easter Day
	65:17-25	C	S. btwn. Nov. 13 and 19, Pr. 28*
	66:1-2	ABC	St. Matthias
	66:10-14	C	S. btwn. July 3 and 9, Pr. 9
Jeremiah			
	1:4-10	C	4 Epiphany
	1:4-10	C	S. btwn. Aug. 21 and 27, Pr. 16*
	2:4-13	C	S. btwn. Aug. 28 and Sept. 3, Pr. 17*
	4:11-12, 22-28	C	S. btwn. Sept. 11 and 17, Pr. 19*
	8:18—9:1	C	S. btwn. Sept. 18 and 24, Pr. 20*
	11:18-20	B	S. btwn. Sept. 18 and 24, Pr. 20
	14:7-10, 19-22	C	S. btwn. Oct. 23 and 29, Pr. 25
	15:15-21	A	S. btwn. Aug. 28 and Sept. 3, Pr. 17
	17:5-10	C	6 Epiphany
	18:1-11	C	S. btwn. Sept. 4 and 10, Pr. 18*
	20:7-13	A	S. btwn. June 19 and 25, Pr. 7
	23:1-6	C	Christ the King, Pr. 29
	23:1-6	C	Christ the King, Pr. 29*
	23:1-6	B	S. btwn. July 17 and 23, Pr. 11
	23:23-29	C	S. btwn. Aug. 14 and 20, Pr. 15
	26:[1-6] 7-16	ABC	St. Simon and St. Jude
	28:5-9	A	S. btwn. June 26 and July 2, Pr. 8
	29:1, 4-7	C	S. btwn. Oct. 9 and 15, Pr. 23*
	31:1-6	A	Easter Day
	31:7-9	B	S. btwn. Oct. 23 and 29, Pr. 25
	31:7-14	ABC	2 Christmas
	31:15-17	ABC	Holy Innocents
	31:27-34	C	S. btwn. Oct. 16 and 22, Pr. 24*
	31:31-34	B	5 Lent
	31:31-34	ABC	Reformation Day
	32:1-3a, 6-15	C	S. btwn. Sept. 25 and Oct. 1, Pr. 21*
	33:14-16	C	1 Advent
Lamentations			
	1:1-6	C	S. btwn. Oct. 2 and 8, Pr. 22*
	3:1-9, 19-24	ABC	Holy Saturday

RCL | Lesser Festival reading		Year	RCL* | Lesser Festival
(Lam.)	3:19-26	C	S. btwn. Oct. 2 and 8, Pr. 22*
	3:22-33	B	S. btwn. June 26 and July 2, Pr. 8
Ezekiel			
	2:1-5	B	S. btwn. July 3 and 9, Pr. 9
	2:8—3:11	ABC	St. Matthew
	3:16-21	ABC	St. Andrew
	17:22-24	B	S. btwn. June 12 and 18, Pr. 6
	18:1-4, 25-32	A	S. btwn. Sept. 25 and Oct. 1, Pr. 21
	33:7-11	A	S. btwn. Sept. 4 and 10, Pr. 18
	34:11-16	ABC	St. Peter and St. Paul
	34:11-16, 20-24	A	Christ the King, Pr. 29
	36:24-28	ABC	Vigil of Easter
	37:1-14	A	5 Lent
	37:1-14	B	Day of Pentecost
	37:1-14	ABC	Vigil of Easter
Daniel			
	3:1-29	ABC	Vigil of Easter
	7:1-3, 15-18	C	All Saints Day
	7:9-10, 13-14	B	Christ the King, Pr. 29
	10:10-14; 12:1-3	ABC	St. Michael and All Angels
	12:1-3	B	S. btwn. Nov. 13 and 19, Pr. 28
Hosea			
	1:2-10	C	S. btwn. July 24 and 30, Pr. 12*
	2:14-20	B	8 Epiphany
	2:14-20	B	S. btwn. May 24 and 28, Pr. 3
	5:15—6:6	A	S. btwn. June 5 and 11, Pr. 5
	11:1-11	C	S. btwn. July 31 and Aug. 6, Pr. 13*
Joel			
	2:1-2, 12-17	ABC	Ash Wednesday
	2:21-27	B	Thanksgiving Day
	2:23-32	C	S. btwn. Oct. 23 and 29, Pr. 25*
Amos			
	5:6-7, 10-15	B	S. btwn. Oct. 9 and 15, Pr. 23
	5:18-24	A	S. btwn. Nov. 6 and 12, Pr. 27
	6:1a, 4-7	C	S. btwn. Sept. 25 and Oct. 1, Pr. 21
	7:7-15	B	S. btwn. July 10 and 16, Pr. 10
	7:7-17	C	S. btwn. July 10 and 16, Pr. 10*
	8:1-12	C	S. btwn. July 17 and 23, Pr. 11*
	8:4-7	C	S. btwn. Sept. 18 and 24, Pr. 20
Jonah			
	2:1-3 [4-6] 7-9	ABC	Vigil of Easter

RCL | Lesser Festival reading	Year	RCL* | Lesser Festival
(Jonah) 3:1-5, 10	B	3 Epiphany
3:1—10	ABC	Vigil of Easter
3:10—4:11	A	S. btwn. Sept. 18 and 24, Pr. 20
Micah		
3:5-12	A	S. btwn. Oct. 30 and Nov. 5, Pr. 26
5:2-5a	C	4 Advent
6:1-8	A	4 Epiphany
Habakkuk		
1:1-4; 2:1-4	C	S. btwn. Oct. 2 and 8, Pr. 22
1:1-4; 2:1-4	C	S. btwn. Oct. 30 and Nov. 5, Pr. 26*
Zephaniah		
1:7, 12-18	A	S. btwn. Nov. 13 and 19, Pr. 28
3:14-20	C	3 Advent
3:14-20	ABC	Vigil of Easter
Haggai		
1:15b—2:9	C	S. btwn. Nov. 6 and 12, Pr. 27*
Zechariah		
9:9-12	A	S. btwn. July 3 and 9, Pr. 9
Malachi		
3:1-4	ABC	Nativity of St. the Baptist
3:1-4	ABC	Presentation of Our Lord
3:1-4	C	2 Advent
4:1-2a	C	S. btwn. Nov. 13 and 19, Pr. 28
Wisdom of Solomon		
1:13-15; 2:23-24	B	S. btwn. June 26 and July 2, Pr. 8
1:16—2:1, 12-22	B	S. btwn. Sept. 18 and 24, Pr. 20
3:1-9	B	All Saints Day
6:12-16	A	S. btwn. Nov. 6 and 12, Pr. 27
6:17-20	A	S. btwn. Nov. 6 and 12, Pr. 27
7:26—8:1	B	S. btwn. Sept. 11 and 17, Pr. 19*
10:15-21	ABC	2 Christmas
12:13, 16-19	A	S. btwn. July 17 and 23, Pr. 11
Sirach		
10:12-18	C	S. btwn. Aug. 28 and Sept. 3, Pr. 17
15:15-20	A	6 Epiphany
24:1-12	ABC	2 Christmas
27:4-7	C	S. btwn. May 24 and 28, Pr. 3
27:4-7	C	8 Epiphany
35:12-17	C	S. btwn. Oct. 23 and 29, Pr. 25

RCL	Lesser Festival reading	Year	RCL*	Lesser Festival
Baruch		
3:9-15, 32—4:4	ABC	Vigil of Easter
5:1-9	C	2 Advent
Song of the Three Young Men		
35-65	ABC	Vigil of Easter
Matthew		
1:18-25	A	4 Advent
2:1-12	ABC	Epiphany of Our Lord
2:13-18	ABC	Holy Innocents
2:13-23	A	1 Christmas
3:1-12	A	2 Advent
3:13-17	A	Baptism of Our Lord
4:1-11	A	1 Lent
4:12-23	A	3 Epiphany
5:1-12	A	4 Epiphany
5:1-12	A	All Saints Day
5:13-20	A	5 Epiphany
5:21-37	A	6 Epiphany
5:38-48	A	7 Epiphany
6:1-6, 16-21	ABC	Ash Wednesday
6:24-34	A	8 Epiphany
6:24-34	A	S. btwn. May 24 and 28, Pr. 3
6:25-33	B	Thanksgiving Day
7:21-29	A	S. btwn. May 29 and June 4, Pr. 4
9:9-13	ABC	St. Matthew
9:9-13, 18-26	A	S. btwn. June 5 and 11, Pr. 5
9:35—10:8 [9-23]	A	S. btwn. June 12 and 18, Pr. 6
10:7-16	ABC	St. Barnabas
10:24-39	A	S. btwn. June 19 and 25, Pr. 7
10:40-42	A	S. btwn. June 26 and July 2, Pr. 8
11:2-11	A	3 Advent
11:16-19, 25-30	A	S. btwn. July 3 and 9, Pr. 9
13:1-9, 18-23	A	S. btwn. July 10 and 16, Pr. 10
13:24-30, 36-43	A	S. btwn. July 17 and 23, Pr. 11
13:31-33, 44-52	A	S. btwn. July 24 and 30, Pr. 12
14:13-21	A	S. btwn. July 31 and Aug. 6, Pr. 13
14:22-33	A	S. btwn. Aug. 7 and 13, Pr. 14
15:[10-20] 21-28	A	S. btwn. Aug. 14 and 20, Pr. 15
16:13-19	ABC	Confession of St. Peter
16:13-20	A	S. btwn. Aug. 21 and 27, Pr. 16
16:21-28	A	S. btwn. Aug. 28 and Sept. 3, Pr. 17
17:1-9	A	Transfiguration of Our Lord
18:15-20	A	S. btwn. Sept. 4 and 10, Pr. 18
18:21-35	A	S. btwn. Sept. 11 and 17, Pr. 19
20:1-16	A	S. btwn. Sept. 18 and 24, Pr. 20

RCL | Lesser Festival reading	Year	RCL* | Lesser Festival
(Matt.) 21:1-11	A	Sunday of the Passion (palms)
21:23-32	A	S. btwn. Sept. 25 and Oct. 1, Pr. 21
21:33-46	A	S. btwn. Oct. 2 and 8, Pr. 22
22:1-14	A	S. btwn. Oct. 9 and 15, Pr. 23
22:15-22	A	S. btwn. Oct. 16 and 22, Pr. 24
22:34-46	A	S. btwn. Oct. 23 and 29, Pr. 25
23:1-12	A	S. btwn. Oct. 30 and Nov. 5, Pr. 26
23:34-39	ABC	St. Stephen
24:36-44	A	1 Advent
25:1-13	A	S. btwn. Nov. 6 and 12, Pr. 27
25:14-30	A	S. btwn. Nov. 13 and 19, Pr. 28
25:31-46	A	Christ the King, Pr. 29
25:31-46	ABC	New Year's Eve
26:14—27:66	A	Sunday of the Passion
27:11-54	A	Sunday of the Passion
27:57-66	ABC	Holy Saturday
28:1-10	A	Easter Day
28:1-10	A	Vigil of Easter
28:16-20	A	Holy Trinity
Mark		
1:1-8	B	2 Advent
1:1-15	ABC	St. Mark
1:4-11	B	Baptism of Our Lord
1:9-15	B	1 Lent
1:14-20	B	3 Epiphany
1:21-28	B	4 Epiphany
1:29-39	B	5 Epiphany
1:40-45	B	6 Epiphany
2:1-12	B	7 Epiphany
2:13-22	B	8 Epiphany
2:13-22	B	S. btwn. May 24 and 28, Pr. 3
2:23—3:6	B	S. btwn. May 29 and June 4, Pr. 4
3:20-35	B	S. btwn. June 5 and 11, Pr. 5
4:26-34	B	S. btwn. June 12 and 18, Pr. 6
4:35-41	B	S. btwn. June 19 and 25, Pr. 7
5:21-43	B	S. btwn. June 26 and July 2, Pr. 8
6:1-13	B	S. btwn. July 3 and 9, Pr. 9
6:14-29	B	S. btwn. July 10 and 16, Pr. 10
6:30-34, 53-56	B	S. btwn. July 17 and 23, Pr. 11
7:1-8, 14-15, 21-23	B	S. btwn. Aug. 28 and Sept. 3, Pr. 17
7:24-37	B	S. btwn. Sept. 4 and 10, Pr. 18
8:27-35	ABC	St. Peter and St. Paul
8:27-38	B	S. btwn. Sept. 11 and 17, Pr. 19
8:31-38	B	2 Lent
9:2-9	B	Transfiguration of Our Lord

RCL | Lesser Festival reading	Year	RCL* | Lesser Festival
(Mark) 9:30-37	B	S. btwn. Sept. 18 and 24, Pr. 20
9:38-50	B	S. btwn. Sept. 25 and Oct. 1, Pr. 21
10:2-16	B	S. btwn. Oct. 2 and 8, Pr. 22
10:17-31	B	S. btwn. Oct. 9 and 15, Pr. 23
10:35-45	B	S. btwn. Oct. 16 and 22, Pr. 24
10:35-45	ABC	St. James the Elder
10:46-52	B	S. btwn. Oct. 23 and 29, Pr. 25
11:1-11	B	Sunday of the Passion (palms)
12:28-34	B	S. btwn. Oct. 30 and Nov. 5, Pr. 26
12:38-44	B	S. btwn. Nov. 6 and 12, Pr. 27
13:1-8	B	S. btwn. Nov. 13 and 19, Pr. 28
13:24-37	B	1 Advent
14:1—15:47	B	Sunday of the Passion
15:1-39 [40-47]	B	Sunday of the Passion
16:1-8	B	Easter Day
16:1-8	B	Vigil of Easter
Luke		
1:1-4; 24:44-53	ABC	St. Luke
1:26-38	B	4 Advent
1:26-38	ABC	Annunciation of Our Lord
1:39-45 [46-55]	C	4 Advent
1:39-57	ABC	Visitation
1:46-55	ABC	Mary, Mother of Our Lord
1:47-55	A, B	3 Advent
1:47-55	B, C	4 Advent
1:57-67 [68-80]	ABC	Nativity of St. the Baptist
1:68-79	C	2 Advent
1:68-79	C	Christ the King, Pr. 29
2:[1-7] 8-20	ABC	Christmas Dawn (II)
2:1-14 [15-20]	ABC	Christmas Eve (I)
2:15-21	ABC	Name of Jesus
2:22-40	B	1 Christmas
2:22-40	ABC	Presentation of Our Lord
2:41-52	C	1 Christmas
3:1-6	C	2 Advent
3:7-18	C	3 Advent
3:15-17, 21-22	C	Baptism of Our Lord
4:1-13	C	1 Lent
4:14-21	C	3 Epiphany
4:21-30	C	4 Epiphany
5:1-11	C	5 Epiphany
6:12-16	ABC	St. Matthias
6:17-26	C	6 Epiphany
6:20-31	C	All Saints Day
6:27-38	C	7 Epiphany

RCL	Lesser Festival reading	Year	RCL*	Lesser Festival
(Luke)	6:39-49	C		8 Epiphany
	6:39-49	C		S. btwn. May 24 and 28, Pr. 3
	7:1-10	C		S. btwn. May 29 and June 4, Pr. 4
	7:11-17	C		S. btwn. June 5 and 11, Pr. 5
	7:36—8:3	C		S. btwn. June 12 and 18, Pr. 6
	8:26-39	C		S. btwn. June 19 and 25, Pr. 7
	9:28-36 [37-43]	C		Transfiguration of Our Lord
	9:51-62	C		S. btwn. June 26 and July 2, Pr. 8
	10:1-11, 16-20	C		S. btwn. July 3 and 9, Pr. 9
	10:17-20	ABC		St. Michael and All Angels
	10:25-37	C		S. btwn. July 10 and 16, Pr. 10
	10:38-42	C		S. btwn. July 17 and 23, Pr. 11
	11:1-13	C		S. btwn. July 24 and 30, Pr. 12
	12:13-21	C		S. btwn. July 31 and Aug. 6, Pr. 13
	12:32-40	C		S. btwn. Aug. 7 and 13, Pr. 14
	12:49-56	C		S. btwn. Aug. 14 and 20, Pr. 15
	13:1-9	C		3 Lent
	13:10-17	C		S. btwn. Aug. 21 and 27, Pr. 16
	13:31-35	C		2 Lent
	14:1, 7-14	C		S. btwn. Aug. 28 and Sept. 3, Pr. 17
	14:25-33	C		S. btwn. Sept. 4 and 10, Pr. 18
	15:1-3, 11b-32	C		4 Lent
	15:1-10	C		S. btwn. Sept. 11 and 17, Pr. 19
	16:1-13	C		S. btwn. Sept. 18 and 24, Pr. 20
	16:19-31	C		S. btwn. Sept. 25 and Oct. 1, Pr. 21
	17:5-10	C		S. btwn. Oct. 2 and 8, Pr. 22
	17:11-19	C		S. btwn. Oct. 9 and 15, Pr. 23
	17:11-19	A		Thanksgiving Day
	18:1-8	C		S. btwn. Oct. 16 and 22, Pr. 24
	18:9-14	C		S. btwn. Oct. 23 and 29, Pr. 25
	19:1-10	C		S. btwn. Oct. 30 and Nov. 5, Pr. 26
	19:28-40	C		Sunday of the Passion
	20:27-38	C		S. btwn. Nov. 6 and 12, Pr. 27
	21:5-19	C		S. btwn. Nov. 13 and 19, Pr. 28
	21:10-19	ABC		Conversion of St. Paul
	21:25-36	C		1 Advent
	22:14—23:56	C		Sunday of the Passion
	23:1-49	C		Sunday of the Passion
	23:33-43	C		Christ the King, Pr. 29
	24:1-12	C		Vigil of Easter
	24:1-12	C		Easter Day
	24:13-35	A		3 Easter
	24:13-49	ABC		Easter Evening
	24:36b-48	B		3 Easter
	24:44-53	ABC		Ascension of Our Lord

RCL | Lesser Festival reading	Year	RCL* | Lesser Festival
John		
1:[1-9] 10-18	ABC	2 Christmas
1:1-14	ABC	Christmas Day (III)
1:6-8, 19-28	B	3 Advent
1:29-42	A	2 Epiphany
1:35-42	ABC	St. Andrew
1:43-51	B	2 Epiphany
1:43-51	ABC	St. Bartholomew
2:1-11	C	2 Epiphany
2:13-22	B	3 Lent
3:1-17	A	2 Lent
3:1-17	B	Holy Trinity
3:13-17	ABC	Holy Cross Day
3:14-21	B	4 Lent
4:5-42	A	3 Lent
5:1-9	C	6 Easter
6:1-21	B	S. btwn. July 24 and 30, Pr. 12
6:24-35	B	S. btwn. July 31 and Aug. 6, Pr. 13
6:25-35	C	Thanksgiving Day
6:35, 41-51	B	S. btwn. Aug. 7 and 13, Pr. 14
6:51-58	B	S. btwn. Aug. 14 and 20, Pr. 15
6:56-69	B	S. btwn. Aug. 21 and 27, Pr. 16
7:37-39	A	Day of Pentecost
7:37-39	ABC	Vigil of Pentecost
8:31-36	ABC	Reformation Day
9:1-41	A	4 Lent
10:1-10	A	4 Easter
10:11-18	B	4 Easter
10:22-30	C	4 Easter
11:1-45	A	5 Lent
11:32-44	B	All Saints Day
12:1-8	C	5 Lent
12:1-11	ABC	Monday after Passion Sunday
12:12-16	B	Sunday of the Passion (palms)
12:20-33	B	5 Lent
12:20-36	ABC	Tuesday in Holy Week
13:1-17, 31b-35	ABC	Maundy Thursday
13:21-32	ABC	Wednesday in Holy Week
13:31-35	C	5 Easter
14:1-7	ABC	St. Thomas
14:1-14	A	5 Easter
14:8-14	ABC	St. Philip and St. James
14:8-17 [25-27]	C	Day of Pentecost
14:15-21	A	6 Easter
14:21-27	ABC	St. Simon and St. Jude

RCL | Lesser Festival reading	Year	RCL* | Lesser Festival
(John) 14:23-29	C	6 Easter
15:1-8	B	5 Easter
15:9-17	B	6 Easter
15:26-27; 16:4b-15	B	Day of Pentecost
16:12-15	C	Holy Trinity
17:1-11	A	7 Easter
17:6-19	B	7 Easter
17:20-26	C	7 Easter
18:1—19:42	ABC	Good Friday
18:33-37	B	Christ the King, Pr. 29
19:38-42	ABC	Holy Saturday
20:1-2, 11-18	ABC	St. Mary Magdalene
20:1-18	ABC	Easter Day
20:19-23	A	Day of Pentecost
20:19-31	ABC	2 Easter
21:1-19	C	3 Easter
21:20-25	ABC	St. John
Acts		
1:1-11	ABC	Ascension of Our Lord
1:6-14	A	7 Easter
1:15-17, 21-26	B	7 Easter
1:15-26	ABC	St. Matthias
2:1-11	ABC	Vigil of Pentecost
2:1-21	ABC	Day of Pentecost
2:14a, 22-32	A	2 Easter
2:14a, 36-41	A	3 Easter
2:42-47	A	4 Easter
3:12-19	B	3 Easter
4:5-12	B	4 Easter
4:8-13	ABC	Confession of St. Peter
4:32-35	B	2 Easter
5:27-32	C	2 Easter
6:8—7:2a, 51-60	ABC	St. Stephen
7:55-60	A	5 Easter
8:14-17	C	Baptism of Our Lord
8:26-40	B	5 Easter
9:1-6 [7-20]	C	3 Easter
9:1-22	ABC	Conversion of St. Paul
9:36-43	C	4 Easter
10:34-43	A	Baptism of Our Lord
10:34-43	ABC	Easter Day
10:44-48	B	6 Easter
11:1-18	C	5 Easter
11:19-30; 13:1-3	ABC	St. Barnabas
11:27—12:3a	ABC	St. James the Elder
13:13-26	ABC	Nativity of St. the Baptist

RCL | Lesser Festival reading	Year	RCL* | Lesser Festival
(Acts) 13:26-33a	ABC	St. Mary Magdalene
16:9-15	C	6 Easter
16:16-34	C	7 Easter
17:22-31	A	6 Easter
19:1-7	B	Baptism of Our Lord
Romans		
1:1-7	A	4 Advent
1:16-17; 3:22b-28 [29-31]	A	S. btwn. May 29 and June 4, Pr. 4
3:19-28	ABC	Reformation Day
4:1-5, 13-17	A	2 Lent
4:13-25	B	2 Lent
4:13-25	A	S. btwn. June 5 and 11, Pr. 5
5:1-5	C	Holy Trinity
5:1-8	A	S. btwn. June 12 and 18, Pr. 6
5:1-11	A	3 Lent
5:12-19	A	1 Lent
6:1b-11	A	S. btwn. June 19 and 25, Pr. 7
6:12-23	A	S. btwn. June 26 and July 2, Pr. 8
6:3-11	ABC	Vigil of Easter
7:15-25a	A	S. btwn. July 3 and 9, Pr. 9
8:1-11	A	S. btwn. July 10 and 16, Pr. 10
8:6-11	A	5 Lent
8:12-17	B	Holy Trinity
8:12-25	A	S. btwn. July 17 and 23, Pr. 11
8:14-17	C	Day of Pentecost
8:14-17, 22-27	ABC	Vigil of Pentecost
8:22-27	B	Day of Pentecost
8:26-39	A	S. btwn. July 24 and 30, Pr. 12
9:1-5	A	S. btwn. July 31 and Aug. 6, Pr. 13
10:5-15	A	S. btwn. Aug. 7 and 13, Pr. 14
10:8b-13	C	1 Lent
10:10-18	ABC	St. Andrew
11:1-2a, 29-32	A	S. btwn. Aug. 14 and 20, Pr. 15
12:1-8	A	S. btwn. Aug. 21 and 27, Pr. 16
12:9-16b	ABC	Visitation
12:9-21	A	S. btwn. Aug. 28 and Sept. 3, Pr. 17
13:8-14	A	S. btwn. Sept. 4 and 10, Pr. 18
13:11-14	A	1 Advent
14:1-12	A	S. btwn. Sept. 11 and 17, Pr. 19
15:4-13	A	2 Advent
16:25-27	B	4 Advent
1 Corinthians		
1:1-9	A	2 Epiphany
1:3-9	B	1 Advent
1:10-18	A	3 Epiphany

RCL	Lesser Festival reading	Year	RCL*	Lesser Festival
(1 Cor.) 1:18-24	ABC	Holy Cross Day
1:18-25	B	3 Lent
1:18-31	A	4 Epiphany
1:18-31	ABC	Tuesday in Holy Week
2:1-12 [13-16]	A	5 Epiphany
3:1-9	A	6 Epiphany
3:10-11, 16-23	A	7 Epiphany
3:16-23	ABC	St. Peter and St. Paul
4:1-5	A	8 Epiphany
4:1-5	A	S. btwn. May 24 and 28, Pr. 3
5:6b-8	ABC	Easter Evening
6:12-20	B	2 Epiphany
7:29-31	B	3 Epiphany
8:1-13	B	4 Epiphany
9:16-23	B	5 Epiphany
9:24-27	B	6 Epiphany
10:1-5	ABC	Confession of St. Peter
10:1-13	C	3 Lent
11:23-26	ABC	Maundy Thursday
12:1-11	C	2 Epiphany
12:3b-13	A	Day of Pentecost
12:12-31a	C	3 Epiphany
12:27-31a	ABC	St. Bartholomew
13:1-13	C	4 Epiphany
15:1-11	C	5 Epiphany
15:1-11	B	Easter Day
15:12-20	C	6 Epiphany
15:19-26	C	Easter Day
15:35-38, 42-50	C	7 Epiphany
15:51-58	C	8 Epiphany
15:51-58	C	S. btwn. May 24 and 28, Pr. 3
2 Corinthians		
1:18-22	B	7 Epiphany
3:1-6	B	8 Epiphany
3:1-6	B	S. btwn. May 24 and 28, Pr. 3
3:12—4:2	C	Transfiguration of Our Lord
4:1-6	ABC	St. Philip and St. James
4:3-6	B	Transfiguration of Our Lord
4:5-12	B	S. btwn. May 29 and June 4, Pr. 4
4:13—5:1	B	S. btwn. June 5 and 11, Pr. 5
5:6-10 [11-13] 14-17	B	S. btwn. June 12 and 18, Pr. 6
5:16-21	C	4 Lent
5:20b—6:10	ABC	Ash Wednesday
6:1-13	B	S. btwn. June 19 and 25, Pr. 7
8:7-15	B	S. btwn. June 26 and July 2, Pr. 8

RCL | Lesser Festival reading		Year	RCL* | Lesser Festival
(2 Cor.)	9:6-15	A	Thanksgiving Day
	12:2-10	B	S. btwn. July 3 and 9, Pr. 9
	13:11-13	A	Holy Trinity
Galatians			
	1:1-12	C	S. btwn. May 29 and June 4, Pr. 4
	1:11-24	ABC	Conversion of St. Paul
	1:11-24	C	S. btwn. June 5 and 11, Pr. 5
	2:15-21	C	S. btwn. June 12 and 18, Pr. 6
	3:23-29	C	S. btwn. June 19 and 25, Pr. 7
	4:4-7	B	1 Christmas
	4:4-7	ABC	Mary, Mother of Our Lord
	4:4-7	ABC	Name of Jesus
	5:1, 13-25	C	S. btwn. June 26 and July 2, Pr. 8
	6:[1-6] 7-16	C	S. btwn. July 3 and 9, Pr. 9
Ephesians			
	1:3-14	ABC	2 Christmas
	1:3-14	B	S. btwn. July 10 and 16, Pr. 10
	1:11-23	C	All Saints Day
	1:15-23	ABC	Ascension of Our Lord
	1:15-23	A	Christ the King, Pr. 29
	2:1-10	B	4 Lent
	2:4-10	ABC	St. Matthew
	2:11-22	B	S. btwn. July 17 and 23, Pr. 11
	3:1-12	ABC	Epiphany of Our Lord
	3:14-21	B	S. btwn. July 24 and 30, Pr. 12
	4:1-16	B	S. btwn. July 31 and Aug. 6, Pr. 13
	4:11-16	ABC	St. Thomas
	4:25—5:2	B	S. btwn. Aug. 7 and 13, Pr. 14
	5:8-14	A	4 Lent
	5:15-20	B	S. btwn. Aug. 14 and 20, Pr. 15
	6:10-20	B	S. btwn. Aug. 21 and 27, Pr. 16
Philippians			
	1:3-11	C	2 Advent
	1:21-30	A	S. btwn. Sept. 18 and 24, Pr. 20
	2:1-13	A	S. btwn. Sept. 25 and Oct. 1, Pr. 21
	2:5-11	ABC	Name of Jesus
	2:5-11	ABC	Sunday of the Passion
	3:4b-14	C	5 Lent
	3:4b-14	A	S. btwn. Oct. 2 and 8, Pr. 22
	3:17—4:1	C	2 Lent
	4:1-9	A	S. btwn. Oct. 9 and 15, Pr. 23
	4:4-7	C	3 Advent
	4:4-9	C	Thanksgiving Day

RCL | Lesser Festival reading	Year	RCL* | Lesser Festival
Colossians		
1:1-14	C	S. btwn. July 10 and 16, Pr. 10
1:11-20	C	Christ the King, Pr. 29
1:15-28	C	S. btwn. July 17 and 23, Pr. 11
2:6-15 [16-19]	C	S. btwn. July 24 and 30, Pr. 12
3:1-4	A	Easter Day
3:1-11	C	S. btwn. July 31 and Aug. 6, Pr. 13
3:12-17	C	1 Christmas
1 Thessalonians		
1:1-10	A	S. btwn. Oct. 16 and 22, Pr. 24
2:1-8	A	S. btwn. Oct. 23 and 29, Pr. 25
2:9-13	A	S. btwn. Oct. 30 and Nov. 5, Pr. 26
3:9-13	C	1 Advent
4:13-18	A	S. btwn. Nov. 6 and 12, Pr. 27
5:1-11	A	S. btwn. Nov. 13 and 19, Pr. 28
5:16-24	B	3 Advent
2 Thessalonians		
1:1-4, 11-12	C	S. btwn. Oct. 30 and Nov. 5, Pr. 26
2:1-5, 13-17	C	S. btwn. Nov. 6 and 12, Pr. 27
3:6-13	C	S. btwn. Nov. 13 and 19, Pr. 28
1 Timothy		
1:12-17	C	S. btwn. Sept. 11 and 17, Pr. 19
2:1-7	C	S. btwn. Sept. 18 and 24, Pr. 20
2:1-7	B	Thanksgiving Day
6:6-19	C	S. btwn. Sept. 25 and Oct. 1, Pr. 21
2 Timothy		
1:1-14	C	S. btwn. Oct. 2 and 8, Pr. 22
2:8-15	C	S. btwn. Oct. 9 and 15, Pr. 23
3:14—4:5	C	S. btwn. Oct. 16 and 22, Pr. 24
4:5-11	ABC	St. Luke
4:6-11, 18	ABC	St. Mark
4:6-8, 16-18	C	S. btwn. Oct. 23 and 29, Pr. 25
Titus		
2:11-14	ABC	Christmas Eve (I)
3:4-7	ABC	Christmas Dawn (II)
Philemon		
1-21	C	S. btwn. Sept. 4 and 10, Pr. 18
Hebrews		
1:1-4 [5-12]	ABC	Christmas Day (III)
1:1-4; 2:5-12	B	S. btwn. Oct. 2 and 8, Pr. 22

RCL | Lesser Festival reading	Year	RCL* | Lesser Festival
(Heb.) 2:10-18	A	1 Christmas
2:14-18	ABC	Presentation of Our Lord
4:12-16	B	S. btwn. Oct. 9 and 15, Pr. 23
4:14-16; 5:7-9	ABC	Good Friday
5:1-10	B	S. btwn. Oct. 16 and 22, Pr. 24
5:5-10	B	5 Lent
7:23-28	B	S. btwn. Oct. 23 and 29, Pr. 25
9:11-14	B	S. btwn. Oct. 30 and Nov. 5, Pr. 26
9:11-15	ABC	Monday after Passion Sunday
9:24-28	B	S. btwn. Nov. 6 and 12, Pr. 27
10:4-10	ABC	Annunciation of Our Lord
10:5-10	C	4 Advent
10:11-14 [15-18] 19-25	B	S. btwn. Nov. 13 and 19, Pr. 28
10:16-25	ABC	Good Friday
11:1-3, 8-16	C	S. btwn. Aug. 7 and 13, Pr. 14
11:29—12:2	C	S. btwn. Aug. 14 and 20, Pr. 15
12:1-3	ABC	Wednesday in Holy Week
12:18-29	C	S. btwn. Aug. 21 and 27, Pr. 16
13:1-8, 15-16	C	S. btwn. Aug. 28 and Sept. 3, Pr. 17
James		
1:17-27	B	S. btwn. Aug. 28 and Sept. 3, Pr. 17
2:1-10 [11-13] 14-17	B	S. btwn. Sept. 4 and 10, Pr. 18
3:1-12	B	S. btwn. Sept. 11 and 17, Pr. 19
3:13—4:3, 7-8a	B	S. btwn. Sept. 18 and 24, Pr. 20
5:7-10	A	3 Advent
5:13-20	B	S. btwn. Sept. 25 and Oct. 1, Pr. 21
1 Peter		
1:3-9	A	2 Easter
1:17-23	A	3 Easter
2:2-10	A	5 Easter
2:19-25	A	4 Easter
3:13-22	A	6 Easter
3:18-22	B	1 Lent
4:1-8	ABC	Holy Saturday
4:12-14; 5:6-11	A	7 Easter
4:12-19	ABC	Holy Innocents
2 Peter		
1:16-21	A	Transfiguration of Our Lord
3:8-15a	B	2 Advent
1 John		
1:1—2:2	ABC	St. John
1:1—2:2	B	2 Easter
3:1-3	A	All Saints Day

137

RCL | Lesser Festival reading	Year	RCL* | Lesser Festival
(1 John) 3:1-7	B	3 Easter
3:16-24	B	4 Easter
4:1-6	ABC	St. Simon and St. Jude
4:7-21	B	5 Easter
5:1-6	B	6 Easter
5:9-13	B	7 Easter
Revelation		
1:4-8	C	2 Easter
1:4b-8	B	Christ the King, Pr. 29
5:11-14	C	3 Easter
7:9-17	C	4 Easter
7:9-17	A	All Saints Day
12:7-12	ABC	St. Michael and All Angels
21:1-6	C	5 Easter
21:1-6a	B	All Saints Day
21:1-6a	ABC	New Year's Eve
21:10, 22—22:5	C	6 Easter
22:12-14, 16-17, 20-21	C	7 Easter

Calendar

	First Sunday in Advent	Baptism of Our Lord	Ash Wednesday	Easter Sunday	Pentecost Sunday	Second Sunday after Pentecost	Christ the King
1998 C	November 30, 1997	January 11	February 25	April 12	May 31	June 14 (Pr. 6)	November 22
1999 A	November 29, 1998	January 10	February 17	April 4	May 23	June 6 (Pr. 5)	November 21
2000 B	November 28, 1999	January 9	March 8	April 23	June 11	June 25 (Pr. 7)	November 26
2001 C	December 3, 2000	January 7	February 28	April 15	June 3	June 17 (Pr. 6)	November 25
2002 A	December 2, 2001	January 13	February 13	March 31	May 19	June 2 (Pr. 4)	November 24
2003 B	December 1, 2002	January 12	March 5	April 20	June 8	June 22 (Pr. 7)	November 23
2004 C	November 30, 2003	January 11	February 25	April 11	May 30	June 13 (Pr. 6)	November 21

CPSIA information can be obtained
at www.ICGtesting.com
Printed in the USA
BVHW01s0120080518
515472BV00013B/31/P